P9-BYF-414

ADDICTIVE THINKING *and*

THE ADDICTIVE PERSONALITY

Two Books in One

Includes:

ADDICTIVE THINKING
Second Edition

BY ABRAHAM J. TWERSKI, M.D.
with a foreword by John Wallace, Ph.D., CAC

THE ADDICTIVE PERSONALITY
Second Edition

BY CRAIG NAKKEN
with a foreword by Damian McElrath, Ph.D.

MJF BOOKS
NEW YORK

Editor's Note: Hazelden offers a variety of information on chemical dependency and related areas. Our publications do not necessarily represent Hazelden's programs, nor do they officially speak for any Twelve Step organization.

Published by MJF Books
Fine Communications
322 Eighth Avenue
New York, NY 10001

Addictive Thinking and The Addictive Personality
Library of Congress Catalog Card Number 99-70057
ISBN 1-56731-331-0

First published 1990, formerly titled *Addictive Thinking: Why Do We Lie to Ourselves? Why Do Others Believe Us?*. Second edition 1997

First published 1988, formerly titled *The Addictive Personality: Roots, Rituals, and Recovery.* Second edition 1996.

This edition published by arrangement with Hazelden Foundation.

Manufactured in the United States of America on acid-free paper

MJF Books and the MJF colophon are trademarks of Fine Creative Media, Inc.

QM 14 13 12 11 10 9 8

ADDICTIVE THINKING

Second Edition

ABRAHAM J. TWERSKI, M.D.

with a foreword by John Wallace, Ph.D., CAC

Contents

Foreword

Few areas of inquiry into human affairs have produced as many experts as the field of chemical dependence. Alcoholism and drug addiction are loaded with international and national experts, each claiming special knowledge of these peculiar diseases that have roused so much controversy while continuing to be so misunderstood by so many. There are experts on wayward chemicals in the brain. Experts who have studied how genes cross the generation gap carrying who knows what cargo of biological risk factors. Experts on family dysfunction. Experts on AA, group therapy, nutrition, behavioral approaches, self-esteem, stress, society and culture, spirituality, relapse, dual diagnoses, and so forth. And while each of these experts undoubtedly holds a piece of the truth about these devastating illnesses, none seems to have as firm a grasp on the whole picture as does Dr. Abraham Twerski.

Dr. Twerski has a marvelous intuitive grasp of the disease of addiction and a knack for portraying real alcoholics in just a few insightful and carefully chosen phrases. Because Dr. Twerski knows these diseases so well, he makes it easy for others to understand them too.

Long before academic psychologists had begun to emerge from the long shadow of a mindless and thoroughgoing behaviorism to reaffirm the importance of such things as reasoning, decision making, concept formation, and so forth, Dr. Twerski was quietly pointing out the critical importance of the cognitive processes of alcoholics and other addicted people and the manner in which these processes enter into their behavior. He has shown that if we are ever to come to grips with the seeming illogic of addicted behavior, we must first come to terms with the various "logics" of addicted thinking. Those of us who operate as change agents with addicted people and their family members must learn how to spot the resistance to change associated with addictive thinking, how to present our clients with the evidence of their peculiar and self-defeating logic, and how to use this evidence in helping people to achieve abstinence and ongoing stable recovery. This book helps us do so.

This new edition of a classic work is a *tour de force* in addictive thinking and its ramifications in all aspects of addictive diseases and recovery from them. In this compact and concisely written volume, Dr. Twerski zeros in on the critical aspects of addictive thinking, and, in an admirable economy of words and phrases, explains addictive thinking, shows it to us clearly through carefully selected examples from his clinical practice and general observations, examines its origins, and explores the importance of such thinking in a host of matters including conflict, guilt, shame, anger, managing feelings, defenses, spirituality, and codependency.

In this current age of the information explosion, when we can be readily overwhelmed by more information than we can possibly absorb in several lifetimes, we are often left to grope about in darkness for some usable knowledge. And even if we do manage to find some reliable knowledge in all the chaff we call data, we are still often left grasping for wisdom and analysis. Happily, Dr. Twerski, in this most welcome new edition of *Addictive Thinking*, manages to give us both. Most readers will come away from reading this book better informed, more knowledgeable about alcoholics and other addicts, and a bit wiser.

JOHN WALLACE, PH.D., CAC

1

What Is Addictive Thinking?

Interviewing Ray, a young man who had been admitted to a rehabilitation unit for drug addiction, I asked, "What made you decide it was time to do something about the problem?"

"I've been on cocaine for a few years," Ray replied, "and occasionally I'd quit using for a few weeks at a time, but I'd never decided to stop for good before.

"For the past year my wife has been pressuring me to stop completely. She used to do cocaine too, but she's been off for several years now. I finally got to the point where doing coke wasn't worth the hassle, so I decided to give it up completely.

"I sincerely wanted to stop for good, but after two weeks I started up again, and that proved something to me. I'm not stupid. I now know that it is absolutely impossible for me to stop on my own, maybe."

I repeated Ray's last sentence several times because I wanted him to hear what he had just said. But he could not see what I was trying to point out.

I said, "It is perfectly logical to say, 'Maybe I can stop by myself.' It is also perfectly logical to say, 'It is absolutely impossible for me to stop by myself.' But to say, 'I now know that it is *absolutely impossible* for me to stop on my own, *maybe,*' is absurd because it is self-contradictory. It is either 'absolutely impossible' or 'maybe,' but it cannot be both." Ray, however, was unable to see my point.

I have repeated this conversation to a number of people, and even seasoned therapists initially show no reaction, waiting for the punch line. Only after I point out the contradiction between "absolutely impossible" and "maybe" do they see the absurdity of the statement and the distortion of thought taking place in this man's mind.

Distortion of Thought

The phenomenon of abnormal thinking in addiction was first recognized in Alcoholics Anonymous, where the highly descriptive term *stinkin' thinkin'* was coined. Old-timers in AA use this term to describe the "dry drunk," or the alcoholic who abstains from drinking but behaves in many other ways much like an active drinker.

Distortions of thinking are not unique to addictive disorders, however; nor are they necessarily related to chemical use at all. Thought distortions can be found in people who may have other adjustment problems. For example, one young woman was procrastinating turning in her term paper for a class.

"Why don't you finish it?" I asked.

"It's finished already," she said.

"Then why haven't you submitted it?" I asked.

"Because I need to do some more work on it," she said.

"But I thought you said it's finished," I remarked.

"It is," she said.

While her assertion appears illogical to most people, it can make perfect sense to someone who thinks addictively. Furthermore, although distorted thinking does not necessarily indicate addiction, the intensity and regularity of this type of thinking are most common among addicts.

We all recognize that the statements "The term paper is all finished" and "I have to do more work on it" are contradictory. But Ray's statement, "I now know that it is absolutely impossible for me to stop on my own, maybe," may not appear absurd until we stop to analyze it. In normal conversation, we generally do not have time to pause and analyze what we hear. Hence, we may be deceived by, and accept as reasonable, statements that are meaningless.

Sometimes these contradictions can be even more subtle. For example, a woman, asked whether she had resolved all the conflicts connected with her divorce, answered, "I think so." There is nothing patently absurd about this woman's answer, until we pause to analyze it. The question "Have you resolved the conflicts?" means "Have you done away with the various uncertainties and eliminated the emotional problems incidental to your divorce?" That is what the word *resolved* means. The answer "I think so" is thus an assertion "I am still uncertain that I am certain" and is really meaningless.

Thinking Processes in Schizophrenia

To understand more fully what we are talking about when we use the term *distortion of thought*, let's look at an extreme example of it, the system of thinking used by a schizophrenic person. As absurd as a particular distorted thought may be to a healthy person, it may make perfect sense to a schizophrenic.

Therapists familiar with paranoid schizophrenic patients who have delusions of grandeur know how futile it is trying to convince a patient that he or she is not the Messiah or the victim of worldwide conspiracy. The therapist and the patient are operating on two totally different wavelengths, with two completely different rules of thought. Normal thinking is as absurd to a schizophrenic as schizophrenic thinking is to a healthy person. A typical schizophrenic's adjustment to life in a normal society can be described in terms of a baseball manager who orders the team to punt or a football coach who calls for stealing a base.

Schizophrenic people do not realize that their thinking processes are different from the thinking processes of most other people. They can't see why others refuse to recognize them as the Messiah or the victim of a worldwide conspiracy.

Still, many people, some therapists included, may argue with a schizophrenic person and then become frustrated when the person fails to see the validity of their arguments. But this is like asking a color-blind person to distinguish colors.

Yet the thinking of the schizophrenic is so obviously irrational that most of us clearly recognize it as such. We may not be able to communicate effectively with a schizophrenic person, but at least we are not fooled by the delusions created in the schizophrenic's mind. We are more frequently taken in by the relative subtlety of distortions caused by addictive thinking.

How Addictive Diseases Resemble Schizophrenia

Sometimes people with addictive diseases are misdiagnosed as schizophrenic. They may have some of the same symptoms, including

- delusions
- hallucinations
- inappropriate moods
- very abnormal behavior

All of these symptoms, however, may be manifestations of the toxic effects of chemicals on the brain. These people have what is called a chemically induced psychosis, which may resemble but is not schizophrenia. These symptoms usually disappear after the chemical toxicity is alleviated and the brain chemistry returns to normal.

A person with schizophrenia, however, may also use alcohol or other drugs addictively. This presents a very difficult treatment problem. A schizophrenic is likely to require long-term maintenance on potent antipsychotic medications. Furthermore, a person with schizophrenia may not be able to tolerate the confrontational techniques commonly effective with addicts in treatment. Therapists teach addicts to desist from escapism and to use their skills to cope effectively with reality. No such demands can be made on a schizophrenic, who may actually lack the ability to cope with reality.

In a sense, both the addict and the schizophrenic are like derailed trains. With some effort, an addict can be put back onto the track. The schizophrenic, however, can't be put back on the same track. The best that may be accomplished is getting this person on another track that leads to the destination. This other track is not a "through" track. It has countless junctions and turnoffs, and at any point the schizophrenic may go off in a direction other than the desired one. Constant vigilance and guidance are necessary to avoid such turnoffs, and it may be necessary to use medications to slow the traveling speed and stay on track.

Being confronted with the thinking of an alcoholic, or someone with another addiction, can be as frustrating as dealing with the schizophrenic. Just as we are unable to budge the schizophrenic from the conviction of being the Messiah, so we are unable to budge an alcoholic from the belief that he or she is a safe, social drinker, or a safe user of tranquilizers, or a "recreational" user of marijuana and cocaine.

For instance, someone close enough to observe a late-stage alcoholic (or other drug addict) sees a person whose life is steadily falling apart; perhaps the addict's physical health is deteriorating, family life is in ruins, and job is in jeopardy. All of these problems are obviously due to the effects of alcohol or other drugs, yet the addict appears unable to recognize this. He or she may firmly believe that using chemicals has nothing to do with any of these problems and seems blind to logical arguments to the contrary.

A defining difference between addictive thinking and schizophrenic thinking is this:

- schizophrenic thinking is blatantly absurd
- addictive thinking has a superficial logic that can be very seductive and misleading

The addict may not always be as willfully conniving as others think. This person is not necessarily consciously and purposely misleading others, though this does occur sometimes. Often addicts are taken in by their own thinking, actually deceiving themselves.

Especially in the early stages of addiction, an addict's perspective and account of what is happening may look reasonable on the surface. As discussed, many people are naturally taken in by addictive reasoning. Thus, an addict's family may see things the "addictive thinking way" for a long time. The addict may sound convincing to friends, pastor, employer, doctor, or even to a psychotherapist. Each statement the addict makes appears to hold up; long accounts of events may even appear valid.

Obsessions and Compulsions in Addiction and Codependency

The treachery of self-deceptive thinking may infect codependent family members as well as the chemically dependent person. Who is codependent? Various definitions and descriptions of codependency exist, but the one that seems most comprehensive is Melody Beattie's: "A codependent person is one who has let another person's behavior affect him or her, and who is obsessed with controlling that person's behavior."*

The important parts of this definition are the words *obsessed* and *controlling*. Obsessive thoughts crowd out all other thoughts, and they drain mental energy. Obsessive thoughts may intrude at any time, and, strangely enough, any attempt to get rid of obsessive thoughts may only increase their intensity.

Trying to drive away obsessive thoughts is like trying to get a coiled spring out of the way by compressing it. The more pressure exerted against the spring, the harder it eventually recoils.

* Melody Beattie, *Codependent No More* (Center City, Minn.: Hazelden Educational Materials, 1992), 36.

At the risk of oversimplification, we might say that the addicted person is plagued by the *compulsion* to use chemicals. A codependent person has an *obsession* with the addict's use and the need to control the addict.

Obsessions and compulsions are closely related. The term *obsessive-compulsive neurosis* has been used in psychiatry for many years. Both obsession and compulsion are characterized by the person's being preoccupied, even consumed, by something irrational. In an obsessional neurosis, it is an irrational idea that plagues the person. In a compulsive neurosis, it is an irrational act. The reason the two are joined in psychiatry is that in almost every instance where the person is obsessed with an idea, there is some compulsive behavior. In virtually every case of compulsive behavior, there are obsessional thoughts. The following story illustrates how obsessional thoughts work.

The Chair on the Desk

While teaching psychiatry to medical students, I had a student who expressed interest in learning more about hypnosis. I felt that the most effective method of teaching this was to hypnotize him and allow him to learn firsthand what a hypnotic trance is and the various phenomena that can be produced under hypnosis.

This young man happened to be an excellent hypnotic subject, and in several sessions, I was able to demonstrate the various applications of hypnosis. Because I also wanted him to understand the phenomenon of post-hypnotic suggestion, I said to him: "Some time after you emerge from this trance, I will give you a signal—I will tap my pencil on the desk. At that point, you will get up, pick up the chair on which you are sitting, and place it on my desk. However, you will have no memory that I gave this instruction." I then brought him out of the trance, and we continued our discussion about hypnosis.

After several moments, I nonchalantly picked up my pencil and tapped it lightly on the desk, while continuing the conversation. Within a few moments, the student, obviously uncomfortable, began to fidget. "I have this crazy urge to pick up my chair and put it on your desk," he said.

"Why should you want to do that?" I asked.

"I don't know. It's a crazy idea, but I just feel like I have to do it." He paused. "Did you tell me something like that during the trance?"

"Yes, I did."

"Then why can't I remember it?" he asked.

"Because when I gave you the suggestion, I told you that you would not remember it."

"Then I don't have to do it, do I?"

"I guess not," I answered.

Shortly afterward, the student left. About twenty minutes later, the door flew open. The young man burst into my office, picked up the chair, and angrily placed it on the desk. "Damn you!" he said, and turned around and left in a fury.

This is the nature of an obsession or a compulsion, whether it occurs from a suggestion given under hypnosis or from a subconscious urge from some unknown origin. Just as putting a chair on a desk is nonsensical, a compulsive act can be irrational, yet the urge to do it may be virtually irresistible. Trying to resist the urge can produce so much anxiety and discomfort that the individual may give in to it simply to get relief from the intense pressure. With most obsessions and compulsions, this period of relief is quite brief; then the urge recurs, often with even greater force than previously.

Codependent people often behave in these obsessive-compulsive ways when they try to control an addict's behavior or use of chemicals. They may be obsessed with trying to help the addict or, later, if their efforts have failed, with punishing the addict.

How Addiction and Codependency Are Similar

Similarities between the behavior of an addict and the behavior of a codependent are striking. Addicts are usually looking for new ways to continue to use chemicals while trying to avoid their destructive consequences. A person might drink alcohol or use cocaine "only on weekends" or get a measured amount that will give the desired "high" but not enough to result in intoxication. When the efforts at control fail, addicts do not conclude, *I can't control my use.* Instead, they tell themselves, *That method did not work. I must find another method that does work.*

In the same way, codependents will not conclude that since efforts to stop the addict have been futile, there is no way of controlling the addict. Rather, they look for new ways that will work.

Cause and Effect

Does an addict's distorted thinking cause an addiction, or does the distorted thinking result from the addiction? This is a complex question, and cause and effect cannot easily be determined. By the time an addict enters treatment, several cycles of cause and effect have usually occurred, and anyone trying to tell which is which may be caught in a catch-22. In a sense, it doesn't matter whether someone's thought processes contributed to the addiction or whether addictive thinking is a symptom of addiction. In either case, treatment and recovery must begin somewhere. Since active chemical use stands in the way of success in treatment, abstinence must come first. After prolonged abstinence, when the brain again functions more normally, addicts can focus their attention on their addictive thinking.

This book is intended to help the addicted or codependent person identify his or her thinking processes and begin to overcome addictive thinking.

2

Self-Deception and Addictive Thinking

I cannot stress enough the importance of realizing that addicts are taken in by their own distorted thinking and that they are its victims. If we fail to understand this, we may feel frustrated or angry in dealing with the addict.

Often when we hear the old using or drinking stories of recovering addicts, we laugh, because the absurdity of the addictive thinking and behavior can be hilarious. This, however, is a lot like watching someone slip on a banana peel. After the laughter is over, we realize that the person who fell could be seriously hurt. Similarly, while we may laugh at an addict's antics, we should also realize that this person suffered greatly during active addiction and that many people are still suffering in the same way.

Addictive Thinking and Intelligence

Alan, a recovering alcoholic, was oblivious to the effects of his drinking, in spite of what people said to him. Since he drank only beer, he was certain he did not have an alcohol problem.

Eventually Alan became physically sick and could no longer deny that something was wrong. He concluded that by drinking half a case of beer daily, he was consuming too much fluid. So he switched to scotch and soda. When the physical symptoms got worse, he faulted the soda and switched to whiskey and water. As his symptoms got even worse, he eliminated the water.

Is this rational thinking? Of course not. Can it be classified as psychotic thinking? Not by the current definition of *psychotic*, which is a general term for any major mental disorder characterized by derangement of personality and loss of contact with reality. But his thinking was clearly different from normal thinking.

Addictive thinking is not affected by intelligence. People functioning at the highest intellectual levels are as vulnerable to these thinking distortions as anyone else. In fact, people of unusually high intellect often have more intense degrees of addictive thinking. Thus, highly intellectual people may be the most difficult patients to treat.

The Attorney and the Turkey

Christine, a brilliant and highly skilled attorney, adamantly refused to attend AA meetings, lest the exposure of her alcoholism jeopardize her career and standing in the community. But a visit from a grateful client who presented her with a dressed turkey for the forthcoming Thanksgiving Day changed her mind.

Christine recalled leaving her office that afternoon, walking out into a cold rain, carrying the turkey wrapped in butcher paper. Her next memory is coming to, while leaning against a downtown office building, holding a bare turkey under her arm, the paper washed away by the rain. Anyone seeing her would correctly assume she was drunk. Though she publicly appeared in this condition, she was too embarrassed to let someone see her walk into a church for an AA meeting.

Why didn't this woman's brilliant analytical mind prevent her from such absurd reasoning? For the same reason that brilliant people are not immune to psychosis, neurosis, or depression. Once the psychological or physical craving for the chemical exists, it affects a person's thinking in much the same way as a bribe or other personal interest distorts one's judgment. The need for the chemical is so powerful that it directs the person's thought processes to sanction or preserve the drinking or using. That is the function of addictive thinking: to permit the person to continue the destructive habit. The more brilliant a person is, the more ingenious are his or her reasons for drinking, for not being abstinent, and for considering AA or NA worthless organizations.

Addictive thinking is different from logical thinking in that it does not reach a conclusion based on the evidence or the facts of a situation, but just the reverse! The addict begins with the conclusion *"I need a drink"* (or a drug), and then builds a case for that conclusion, whether it is logical or not, and whether or not the facts support it.

Why Children Take Drugs, Why Parents Drink

An understanding of addictive thinking can help explain why some efforts at preventing alcoholism or other drug abuse fail. Most often, scare tactics are ineffective. Despite the well-publicized drug-related deaths of celebrities and extensive media education about the dangers of cocaine and heroin, many people are still enchanted by the drug mystique. The noxious consequences—including the helplessness of the addiction, the enormous financial cost, the legal problems, and the high risk of death—do not always register.

An important insight resulted from the campaign urging young people to "Just Say No" to drugs. When asked what they thought of this idea, a number of adolescents responded, "Why? What else is there?"

Some youngsters who feel locked out of the American dream may turn to drugs as the only type of gratification they believe they can achieve. Others who do have the opportunity for success may lack confidence in their abilities to succeed. Still others may not see why they should deprive themselves of pleasure.

When achieving pleasure or relieving discomfort constitutes the ultimate goal of life, many people, especially youngsters, will turn to chemicals to reach these goals. It is undeniable that mind-altering chemicals may produce a desirable sensation, and to discourage pursuit of this high, we must be able to convince young people that they should sacrifice such pleasure. Since they seem to consider themselves immune to the dangerous effects of drugs, dire warnings are not a deterrent. Telling them to avoid chemicals so that they can grow up to be healthy, productive people who can enjoy life is often met with the spoken or unspoken argument "Why wait? I'm enjoying life right now by drinking."

To further complicate things, our culture thrives on technology that eliminates waiting. We are consumers of microwaves, fax machines, cellular phones, and instant foods. Even if one can envision "happiness" coming later in life, the prevailing ethos of instant gratification makes a long wait intolerable.

To effectively prevent chemical use among young people, we would have to establish (1) ultimate goals in life other than sense gratification and (2) tolerance for delay. Our culture is not likely to embrace these changes. Instead, our culture embraces addictive thinking.

People may have addictive thinking patterns, which block out certain facts, even before they ever use chemicals. Young people contemplating the use of cocaine, for instance, are often taken in by promises of euphoria, ignoring the potentially terrible cost. Thus, addictive thinking cannot be completely blamed on the effects of chemicals on the brain.

Ironically, another characteristic of addictive thinking is that while it distorts the thinking of addicts about themselves, it may not affect their attitudes toward others. Thus, an actively drinking alcoholic parent may be thoroughly frustrated by a son or daughter who cannot understand the destructive effects of drugs. Likewise, a cocaine-using son or daughter cannot understand how a parent could return to drinking after a close brush with death due to the effects of alcohol.

Remember this, for it is important: *Identification of addictive thinking must come from outside the addict.*

Self-Deception in Addictive Thinking

Everyone gets "taken in" by addictive thinking, but the person most affected by it is the one who is doing the deceptive thinking, the addict or the codependent. The following stories illustrate this point.

"Entering Treatment Wouldn't Be Honest"

Martin, a fifty-five-year-old man, consulted me following an intervention on his alcoholism. His ex-wife, four children, boss, and two close friends confronted him with how his excessive drinking was affecting their lives. Martin's boss, for example, threatened to let Martin go because of his dishonest work habits.

The man claimed this intervention had "opened his eyes." Weeks earlier he had had a drunken-driving accident, but still he denied the problem. But when people cared enough for him to try to get him help, he realized he had to stop drinking. In fact, he hadn't had a drink in the ten days since the intervention.

I told Martin his determination was a good beginning toward recovery, but determination alone could not stop his alcoholism. Treatment was absolutely necessary. I gave him the options of either residential or intensive outpatient treatment.

Martin, however, refused to enter a treatment program. Though he certainly didn't want to lose the affection and closeness of his children, or his job, he could not, in good faith, go to treatment. Why? Because he was certain he could now abstain from alcohol without outside help. So, if he entered treatment only to please his family and business partner when he knew he didn't need treatment, it would be dishonest of him, and he was not about to do anything dishonest.

My urge to burst out laughing because of the absurdity of this reasoning was tempered by my compassion for this man who was tragically deceiving himself. In many years of alcoholism, he had frequently lied to his family, friends, and boss. He hadn't been honest for years. But to enter treatment was unthinkable because to do so would be "dishonest." This man actually believed that what prevented him from accepting help was his commitment to honesty! Such is the self-deception of addictive thinking.

"Only a Social Drinker"

Another example of addictive thinking is provided by a skilled cardiologist who drank heavily for years. As time and drinking went on, he began to experience morning-after effects. Although he got to the office and hospital daily, he felt sick until quite late in the morning. Still, he knew that he was "only a social drinker." He believed something was wrong with the way his stomach absorbed alcohol—too much alcohol was remaining in his stomach overnight.

The doctor remembered medical school, where as a student he participated in a study of digestion. He was given measured amounts of food, and forty-five minutes later a tube was passed through his nose into his stomach. His stomach contents were evacuated and submitted to the laboratory for analysis.

"I had become adept at passing a tube down my nose into my stomach," the doctor recalled, "and it occurred to me that this technique could be the answer to my early morning misery. Before going to bed at night, I would pass a tube into my stomach and empty its contents. As I expected, I woke up the next morning feeling much better. I continued this practice every night for six weeks. The only reason I stopped was because the tube irritated my throat so that my larynx almost closed off, and I was afraid I would require a tracheotomy to breathe.

"But not even once," the doctor said, "not once in those six weeks did it ever occur to me that a social drinker doesn't have to pump his stomach every night!"

Self-Deception and Attending Twelve Step Groups

Involvement in a Twelve Step program is extremely important in recovery, yet many people resist Twelve Step programs because of the insistence on total abstinence. Many alcoholics and addicts, however, will deny this reason and convince themselves that they have other, valid reasons for not becoming involved in AA.

One alcoholic said, "I can't go to AA because the meeting is just one block away from my ex's apartment." He conveniently failed to admit that each week there are meetings at over 140 different locations in his community.

The same kind of self-deception occurs in codependency, as the following stories illustrate.

"I Could Never Go to Al-Anon"

The wife of a financial planner consulted me because of her husband's alcoholism. "His drinking has progressively increased. He now comes home from work, sits down in front of the television with his supply of beer, and that's where he wakes up the next morning. So far he has been able to make it to the office every morning, but it's inevitable that before too long he won't show up for work, or he'll come into the office intoxicated, and it will all be out in the open. He's going to lose his job before long."

The woman explained how during the past few years their home life had deteriorated due to the alcoholism. Father and son were no longer talking to each other. The couple had no social life. They no longer had sexual relations.

The financial planner's wife had put up with all the consequences of the alcoholism until now. Since he was on the verge of ruining his career and livelihood, she felt she had to do something.

She had tried to talk to him numerous times, but he refused suggestions for help, believing he had no problem with alcohol. He told her that if she didn't like it, she could leave.

Since neither she nor the son appeared to have any leverage, there was no point in confronting him. The wife believed that if he were confronted, he would continue to refuse help, and he would tell them to leave the home.

Because there did not appear to be any effective approach toward the husband, I suggested the woman begin looking after her own needs and start attending Al-Anon meetings. I also arranged for her to meet Robert, an accountant who was now in successful recovery and whose history had been almost identical to her husband's.

At this meeting, the recovering accountant described how all of his wife's efforts to get him to quit had been futile, and how he had continued drinking until his alcoholism became obvious at work. After being threatened with dismissal, he had come into treatment. He had had a rocky course until he finally stabilized in sobriety.

"My wife is now in Al-Anon," he said. "Perhaps if she had been in Al-Anon earlier, I might have come to my senses sooner, and my recovery could have been a smoother one. I suggest you start going to Al-Anon now, and my wife will be only too happy to take you to your first meeting, even tonight."

The woman shook her head. "Oh, no," she said. "I could never go to Al-Anon."

"Why not?" we asked.

"Because what would happen if someone recognized me and came to the conclusion that my husband was an alcoholic? Why, the word would get around, and my husband would lose all his clients. Who would allow their money to be managed by an alcoholic?"

I was baffled by her remark. "I don't understand something," I said. "You stated that you had put up with all of the problems that the alcoholism was causing. The only reason you consulted me was because you felt that exposure was imminent, that any day now he would walk into the office obviously intoxicated, and that this would result in his suspension. Since this appears imminent, why are you reluctant to go to Al-Anon? From what you said, he is going to hit bottom in a much more serious way if the alcoholism is not arrested. From what Robert is saying, his opinion is that his wife's participation in Al-Anon could actually have forestalled that happening to him."

Regardless of what we both said, the woman held her ground. She could not go to Al-Anon because she felt that would expose the problem. She couldn't see that Al-Anon was the only thing that she could do that might help her avoid the disastrous consequences she feared.

"I Have Nothing in Common with Them"

In another case, the husband of an executive who had relapsed after detoxification called for help. He stated that his wife refused to attend Alcoholics Anonymous. After leaving the hospital, she had gone to several meetings, but she believed that the meetings were not for her. She was different from the other people at the meetings; she believed she had nothing in common with them.

I told the husband that his wife's resistance to AA was not unusual. After all, in AA she would learn that she could not drink again, and this was something that she did not want to hear.

"How are you doing with your Al-Anon program?" I asked.

"I'm not going to Al-Anon," he said. "I went to two meetings, but that program is not for me. I have nothing in common with the people there."

I pointed out to the man that he was parroting his wife's exact words. Although he criticized her for not participating in a recovery program and for feeling that she was different from the other alcoholics, he avoided his own recovery program for the same reason.

The anxiety about change can be so intense that people, like those in our examples, contradict themselves.

Making Changes

How is it that people can so blatantly contradict themselves, yet not be able to recognize it even if it is pointed out? In one word, the answer is denial. Much of the denial in addictive, distorted thinking is due to intense resistance to change. As long as someone denies reality, he or she can continue behaving the same as before. Acceptance of reality might commit him or her to the very difficult process of change.

Often, people have no problem with changes as long as the change occurs in someone else. When the alcoholic says, "I wouldn't have to drink the way I do if my partner were more considerate," he or she is really saying, "I don't need to change. Make my partner change. I'll be just fine then."

Codependents, for example, may eagerly seek help, thinking experts can tell them what to do to stop someone from using

An Experiment: The Difficulty of Making Changes

Just for fun, try the following experiment: Fold your hands across your chest, and then observe the position of your hands. Some people fold the left hand over the right, and others do the reverse.

After noting how you do it, unfold your hands. Now fold them again, but this time in the opposite way; that is, if you normally put your right hand over your left, put your left hand over your right.

You will probably notice how awkward this feels. The old way is normal and relaxing. The new way may seem strange, and you may feel you could never relax in this position.

If a simple change in position of your hands is so uncomfortable, just think how uncomfortable it is to change part of your behavior or lifestyle.

chemicals. They are disappointed when they learn that they can do nothing to alter the addict's behavior, that they are powerless. When the expert suggests that they look at their own behavior and begin to make changes in themselves, they often back away. They are particularly apt to be turned off when people in Al-Anon tell them, "We don't come here to change our spouse. We come here to change ourselves."

"Change myself?" they may respond. "Why should I change myself? I'm not the one who's drinking!"

Distorted Perceptions

Many of the features of addictive thinking can be seen in codependents as well as addicts because they stem from a similar origin: low self-esteem.

Most emotional problems that are not of physical origin are related, in one way or another, to low self-esteem. Low self-esteem refers to the negative feelings people have about themselves that are not justified by fact. In other words, while some people have a distorted self-perception that includes grandiose delusions about themselves, people with low self-esteem have delusions of inferiority, incompetence, and worthlessness. Strangely enough, these feelings of inadequacy are often particularly intense in people who are the most gifted.

If our perceptions of ourselves are incorrect, we will probably be prone to maladjustment. We can only adjust to reality if we have an accurate perception of it. We create a major component of our own reality, and if we have an unrealistic view of ourselves, we have distorted reality.

I have not yet come across any chemically dependent people who did not have feelings of inferiority that antedated their chemical use. Sometimes they feel inadequate or unworthy in every facet of their lives, and sometimes they may feel very competent in their particular area of expertise, but inadequate and unworthy as a human being, a spouse, a partner, or a parent.

Some people react to feelings of low self-esteem by escaping from life's challenges and distresses into chemicals, and some may find a redeeming feeling of worth and adequacy by being the sober and controlling or suffering significant other of a chemically dependent person.

The Rule of the Three Cs

Al-Anon endorses the rule of the Three Cs: You did not CAUSE it, you cannot CONTROL it, and you cannot CURE it. But many people do feel responsible for another's addiction, do try to control it, and do believe that they can cure it.

Sometimes it seems as though the codependent person is thinking, *I am so powerful that I can cause addiction, or control it, or cure it.* This isn't really a genuine feeling of superiority or arrogance. Quite the contrary, such feelings are often a defensive reaction against feelings of inferiority.

Often, the Three Cs are related to openly acknowledged inferiority. For example, the codependent person thinks, *I am the cause of my daughter's addiction because if I had been a better parent, she would have not turned to drugs. If I had provided her with the love and support she needed, she would not have sought chemicals. The addiction is due to my dereliction. If only I were a better person, she would use less or quit.* These feelings are particularly common for the codependent when the other person is in the early phases of addiction.

The self-deceptive features of addictive thinking and codependency have much in common. In both, there are often denial, rationalization, and projection. In both, contradictory ideas can co-exist, and there is fierce resistance to change oneself and a desire to change others. In both, there is a delusion of control, and in both there is, invariably, low self-esteem. Thus, all the features of addictive thinking are present in both, and the only distinguishing feature may be the chemical use.

3

The Addictive Thinker's Concept of Time

"I can quit any time I want."

If there were a contest for the most common sentence used by addicts, this one would win.

Anyone who has observed addicts knows they "stop" countless times and make innumerable resolutions. Abstinence may be for hours, days, or, in some cases, weeks. But, ordinarily, before long the active practice of addiction resumes. This vicious circle may continue for years.

Addicts simply are unable to stop any time they wish. Others can see this, but the addict does not. Family and friends may be bewildered, asking themselves, *How can a person insist that it's possible to stop at anytime when it's obviously not true?* Even seasoned therapists, used to this reasoning, may ask themselves, *How can an intelligent person be so utterly oblivious to reality? How can first-rate intellectuals, women and men with positions of great responsibility, who can analyze and retain scientific data, not add two plus two in regard to their addictive use of chemicals?*

The answer lies in an understanding of addictive thinking. Addicts may not seem as illogical as they first appear if we understand one thing: the addictive thinker's concept of time. Addicts make perfectly good sense to themselves and others when they say, "I can quit any time I want"; an addict simply has a different concept of time than a nonaddict.

For everyone, time is variable. Under certain circumstances, a few minutes can seem an eternity, while under other circumstances, weeks and months appear to have lasted only moments.

Addicts who claim they can quit any time actually believe it is the truth. Why? Because by abstaining for a day or two, the addict has stopped for a "time." Indeed, having often abstained for several days, addicts may wonder why others cannot realize the obvious: They can stop any "time."

You may tell the addict, "No, it's obvious that you cannot stop any time you want to." Your statement and the addict's, although seemingly contradictory, are both true. The key is that each person is using the word *time* differently.

The Future in Minutes and Seconds

For the addict, time may be measured in minutes or even seconds. Certainly in the quest for the effect of a chemical, the addict thinks in terms of minutes. Addicts are intolerant of delay for the sought-after effect. All of the substances addicts use produce their effects within seconds or minutes.

I have promised myself to one day do the following experiment. I will take a large glass jar and fill it with multicolored capsules. Then I will get the word out on the street that I have received a shipment of "stuff" from South America that is better than anything anyone has ever tried. Why, it gives a "high" that is far superior to both heroin and cocaine combined!

"Wow!" addicts will say. "That must cost a lot of money."

"No, that's the best part of it. Two dollars a hit."

"You must be kidding. Two bucks?"

"Honest to God, and it's the greatest."

"Give me a hundred dollars worth."

"Gladly. But there is one thing I must tell you first. The high is the greatest in the world, but it doesn't hit you for forty-eight or seventy-two hours."

"It doesn't what?"

"It takes between two to three days for the high to develop, but then it's simply the greatest you've ever experienced."

The customers will back away. "Who wants that junk. Keep it!"

Addicts tell me they wouldn't buy a drug, regardless of its great effect and of its low cost, if there were a long delay in the onset of its action. Part of addiction is the immediacy of the high. Delay is not within the addict's frame of reference.

The addict does think about the future, but only in terms of moments, not years. When drinking or using other drugs, addicts do think about the consequences: the glow, a feeling of euphoria, relaxation, detachment from the world, and perhaps sleep. These consequences occur within a few seconds or minutes after drinking or using, and these few seconds or minutes are what make up "time" for the addict. Cirrhosis, brain damage, loss of job, loss of family, or other serious consequences come as the result of a long process and are not likely to occur within minutes. So they simply do not exist in the addict's thoughts.

How different is the alcoholic from the smoker, who risks the consequences of serious circulatory problems, heart disease, emphysema, and cancer? The destructive effects of drinking or using other drugs may occur much sooner than those of smoking, but both the drinker and smoker are oblivious to the future. Similarly, people who participate in risky sexual behaviors may be taking serious chances with their health, but again the consequences are in a "future" that is not within their conception of time.

A Culture with an Addict's Concept of Time

We are part of a culture that values the delivery of service in seconds—e-mail, the Internet, and fast-food restaurants all provide nearly instant gratification. We all, in some ways, operate with the addictive concept of time.

We've polluted the air, rivers, and oceans for short-term

gain, disregarding long-range effects. We've destroyed forests and other habitats of endangered species with little regard for turning this world over to future generations. Are we not disregarding the future, very much as the addict does?

Understanding the Way an Addict Thinks

People involved with the Twelve Step program of Alcoholics Anonymous showed me how the misconception of time is prevalent in addictive thinking. Program people like to use the powerful slogans *One day at a time* and *Time takes time* to combat the forces of addictive thinking.

Recovering people intuitively know that one of the ways they must change their "stinkin' thinkin'" is to deal with their distorted concept of time. Most people are comfortable with the idea that one day is a convenient, manageable unit of time. Often, however, people in early recovery must take it five minutes at a time and eventually work up to longer periods.

The idea of time takes time is used to counter the addictive notion that change can happen fast, such as the addict who prays, "Please, God, give me patience, but give it to me right now!"

One of my patients wrote to me: "It is four years since I was taken into your office, utterly beaten, wanting to die, but not having the courage to take my own life. . . . The first two years, the only thing I did right was not drink and go to meetings. . . . I want you to know that it took me four years to finally feel different about myself."

When addicts recognize that part of their downfall was intolerance of delay and become willing to wait for the rewards of sobriety, they are on their way to recovery. If they want "instant" sobriety, they get nowhere.

Old-timers in AA think of their sobriety in terms of twenty-four-hour segments. They celebrate sobriety anniversaries but with great caution because they know it's risky to think in terms of years rather than days. That's one reason many recovering people rely on meditation books that focus on a day-at-a-time approach, such as *Twenty-Four Hours a Day* and *One Day at a Time in Al-Anon.*

One day at a time is not just a clever slogan. It is absolutely necessary for recovery from addiction, as the next two stories illustrate.

"Nine Thousand, Eight Hundred and Thirty-Four Days"

I once asked a friend in recovery how long he had been sober. He reached into his pocket, took out a small diary, and, after fingering the pages, looked up and said, "Nine thousand, eight hundred and thirty-four days."

I asked, "What is that? Twenty-five or thirty years?"

With complete sincerity, he replied, "You know, doctor, I don't really know. Maybe you can afford to think in terms of years. I have to think in terms of days." When this friend, John McHugh, died at age eighty-three after forty-three years of sobriety, on the night before his death he had entered into his diary the number *16,048*.

"Today You Have Been Sober Longer Than I Have"

After an AA meeting once, a woman said to John in admiration, "It must be wonderful to be sober so long."

John smiled and said to her, "You have been sober longer than I have, Elizabeth."

"How can you say that?" Elizabeth said. "I've only been sober two years, and you've been sober nearly forty years."

"What time did you get up today?" John asked.

"Well, I have to be at work at seven, so I got up at five-thirty."

"I didn't get up today until eight, so today you have been sober longer than I have," John said.

When addicts and codependents fully grasp the one-day-at-a-time concept, they have begun their recovery. They must proceed cautiously, however, because a recurrence of time distortion is reason to suspect the possibility of a relapse. The time dimension of thinking is thus an important consideration for both the recovering addict and the professional in understanding and managing addictive diseases.

4

Confusing Cause and Effect

I once heard an AA speaker describe the way he used to think during his drinking days. The absurdity of his thinking was hilarious, and everyone enjoyed a good laugh. There was more laughter when the man suggested that alcoholic thinking is every bit as destructive as alcoholic drinking. To illustrate, the man read the questions from a self-test for alcoholism, substituting the word *thinking* for the word *drinking*. Here is what he read:

Are You an Addictive Thinker?

1. Do you lose time from work due to thinking?
2. Is thinking making your home life unhappy?
3. Have you ever felt remorse after thinking?
4. Have you gotten into financial difficulties as a result of thinking?
5. Does your thinking make you careless of your family's welfare?
6. Has your ambition decreased since thinking?
7. Does thinking cause you to have difficulty sleeping?
8. Has your efficiency decreased since thinking?
9. Is thinking jeopardizing your job or business?
10. Do you think to escape worries or troubles?

The point is that even in the absence of chemicals, distorted, addictive thinking wreaks havoc. Many addictive thinkers come to their conclusions because they reverse ordinary cause and effect. Their judgment becomes distorted, and as a result taking chemicals becomes fully justified. As one recovering alcoholic put it, "I never in my life took a drink unless I had decided it was the right thing to do at the time." Although addictive thinkers turn logic around, they are absolutely convinced that their logic is valid. They not only resist rational arguments to the contrary, but also they cannot understand why others do not see the "obvious."

An Addict's Version of Dyslexia

We might understand this better with a comparison to dyslexia. Some people who have this learning disorder "see" letters reversed in words. You ask them to read the word *cat,* and they may see TAC or CTA. But they are certain they have read it accurately. The problem involves their perception of how the letters are organized. This does not indicate low intelligence; dyslexia can occur in highly intelligent people.

Something similar happens when an addict mentally reverses cause and effect. For example, Felicia claims that she drinks and uses pills because her home life is intolerable. She is telling what she perceives to be the truth. Her husband has withdrawn from her, is unresponsive to her, and makes caustic comments. Her children are ashamed of her and treat her with disrespect. She believes this emotional torture causes her to drink. She says, "When work is over and you know you've already experienced your high for the day, and there's nothing to look forward to, of course you want a few drinks."

We've all seen cartoons of a man complaining to a woman in a bar, "My wife doesn't understand me."

Woman: What doesn't she understand?

Man: She doesn't understand why I drink.

Woman: Why do you drink?

Man: Because my wife doesn't understand me.

The attitude of the family, pressure on the job, insensitivity of an authoritarian boss, callousness of friends, anxiety attacks, headache or nagging backache, a financial squeeze—or any other problem—whatever the addict claims is the reason for using chemicals, the formula is always the same. The fact is that chemicals usually cause the problems, but the addicted person believes that problems cause chemical use.

While Felicia does indeed have the problems she complains about, she fails to recognize her confusion over cause and effect. Her husband's behavior, although unpleasant, is in response to her drinking and pill taking. He cannot communicate meaningfully with her because of her chemical use. The children are angry and ashamed that they cannot invite friends over because they fear her unpredictable antics. They have lost respect for her because of her chemical use.

Just as a dyslexic person has trouble reading until the problems with perception are addressed, an addicted person's perception of reality will continue to be distorted with or without active use of alcohol or other drugs until the addictive thinking process is corrected.

5

Origins of Addictive Thinking

How does addictive thinking develop? Why do some people develop healthy thinking processes and others develop distorted thinking?

We don't have all the answers, because chemical dependency is a complex disease that results from a complex mix of physical, psychological, and social factors. Understanding how addictive thinking develops may be helpful in preventing addictive thinking and hence alcoholism and other drug addiction. However, it is of limited value in treating and reversing addictive thinking.

An Inability to Reason with Oneself

The most convincing theory on how addictive thinking develops was presented in a 1983 article by Dr. David Sedlak.* Sedlak describes addictive thinking as a person's inability to *make consistently healthy decisions in his or her own behalf.* He points out that this is not a moral failure of a person's willpower, but rather a *disease of the will* and inability to use the will. Sedlak stresses that this unique thinking disorder does not affect other kinds of reasoning. Thus, a person who develops a thinking disorder may be intelligent, intuitive, persuasive, and capable of valid philosophical and scientific reasoning. The peculiarity of addictive

* David Sedlak, M.D., "Childhood: Setting the Stage for Addiction in Childhood and Adolescence," in *Adolescent Substance Abuse: A Guide to Prevention and Treatment,* ed. Richard Isralowitz and Mark Singer (New York: Haworth Press, 1983).

thinking, he says, is the inability *to reason with oneself.* This can apply to various emotional and behavioral problems, but is invariably found in addiction: alcoholism, other drug addiction, compulsive gambling, sexual addiction, eating disorders, nicotine addiction, and codependency.

How does this inability to reason with oneself develop? To understand, we must first recognize how the ability to reason develops. According to Sedlak, the ability to reason with oneself requires certain factors. First, a person must have adequate facts about reality. A person who does not know the damage alcohol or other drugs can do cannot reason correctly about their use.

Second, a person must have certain values and principles as grounds for making choices. People develop values and principles from their culture as well as from their home. For instance, a young man growing up with family or cultural values that say that a man proves his masculinity by being able to hold his liquor may be expected to drink excessively. Failure to live up to these expectations can generate deep disappointment.

Third, the person must develop a healthy and undistorted self-concept. The psychiatrist Silvano Arieti suggests that small children feel extremely insecure and threatened in a huge and overwhelming world. A major source of children's security is reliance on adults, primarily parents. If children think their parents or other significant adults are irrational, unjust, and arbitrary, the anxiety is intolerable. Therefore, children must maintain, at whatever cost, a conviction that the world is fair, just, and rational.

In truth, the world is often neither fair, nor just, nor rational. Children, however, cannot see it this way. They conclude instead that because the world "must be fair, just, and rational" their perception is faulty. They think, *I must not be able to judge things correctly. I am stupid.*

Similarly, even if children are abused or unfairly punished, they may be unable to believe, *My parents are crazy. They punish me for no good reason.* This would be too terrifying a concept to tolerate. To preserve the notion that their parents are rational and predictable, their only option is to conclude, *I must somehow be bad to have been punished this way.*

Finally, we enter the world as helpless infants, incapable of doing many things that grownups can do. With good parenting and a propitious environment, we overcome much of this sense of helplessness as we grow.

Sometimes parents demand things of young children which they are incapable of doing. Children may feel that they should be able to do what their parents ask, and the fact that they are unable to do so may cause them to feel inadequate. On the other hand, parents can do too much for their children, not allowing their children to flex their own muscles. Such children have no chance of developing self-confidence. Successful parenting requires a knowledge of what a child can and cannot do at various stages of development, and parents should encourage their children to use their capacities.

Parents are encouraged to take an interest in the child's schoolwork, even to assist in homework. However, when parents do the homework for the child, they reinforce the child's conviction that he or she is unable to do it. Incidentally, when parents do much for the child that he or she can do alone, they are acting codependently. A child who says, "I can't do word problems," and is allowed to get away with it, actually has the feeling of inadequacy reconfirmed.

As children grow up, these misconceptions may continue to color their thinking and behavior. They may continue to feel that they are bad people and undeserving of good things. Or they may consider their judgment grossly defective, which allows others to sway them easily.

A person can feel bad or worthless, even though this totally contradicts reality. Feeling insecure and inadequate makes a person more vulnerable to escapism, so often accomplished via mood-altering drugs. The person feels different from the rest of the world, as if he or she doesn't belong anywhere. Alcohol or other drugs, or other objects of addiction, anesthetize the pain and allow this person to feel part of the "normal world." Indeed, many alcoholics or other addicts state they did not seek a "high," but only to feel normal.

Many thinking distortions are not necessarily related to chemical use. For example, fear of rejection, anxiety, isolation, and despair often result from low self-esteem. Many of the quirks of addictive thinking are psychological defenses against these painful feelings, and these symptoms are due to the persistence of the distorted self-image that began in childhood.

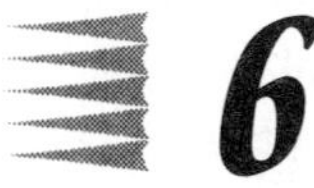

6

Denial, Rationalization, and Projection

The three most common elements in addictive thinking are (1) denial, (2) rationalization, and (3) projection. Although people familiar with treatment of addictions are aware of the prevalence of these traits in addicts, there is nonetheless good reason for us to explore them in more detail. Progressive elimination of these distortions is a key to the recovering addict's making improvements.

The term *denial* as used here could be misunderstood. Ordinarily, denying something that actually happened is thought of as lying. While addictive behavior does include lying, denial in addictive thinking does not mean telling lies. Lying is a willful and conscious distortion of facts or concealment of truth. A liar is aware of lying. The denial of an addictive thinker is neither conscious nor willful, and the addict may sincerely believe that he or she is telling the truth.

Denial and, for that matter, rationalization and projection are unconscious mechanisms. While they are often gross distortions of truth, they are the truth to the addict. The addict's behavior can be understood only in the light of the unconscious nature of these mechanisms. This is why confronting the denial, rationalization, and projection with facts to the contrary is ineffective.

Some phobias are the result of faulty perception. For example, a young boy who is frightened by a dog may develop a fear of dogs and many years later, as a man, may have a panic reaction when a harmless little puppy approaches him. Although physically he sees a tiny puppy, the psychological perception is that of a ferocious dog about to attack him. In other words, while the conscious perception is that of a puppy, the unconscious perception is that of a monster. Emotional responses are often related to the unconscious rather than to the conscious perception.

The Role of Faulty Perceptions

Addicts react according to their unconscious perceptions. If these perceptions were valid, their behavior would be perfectly understandable. Unless we can show them that their perception is faulty, we cannot expect their reactions and behavior to change.

Given how important the self-concept is in addictive disease, the addict's distorted self-perception is the biggest problem. All other distorted perceptions are actually secondary.

Virtually all of an addict's defense mechanisms are unconscious, and their function is to protect the addict from some intolerable, unacceptable, and catastrophic awareness.

That psychological defense mechanisms can operate without conscious awareness should not be surprising. Certainly physical defenses work without cognitive awareness of their function. For example, when we sustain injury, even a tiny cut, our system goes into a defensive posture to prevent the injury from threatening our life. White blood cells from remote parts of the body destroy bacteria that enter the wound, and the bone marrow promptly begins to produce tens of thousands more white blood cells to fight infection. The platelets and other blood-coagulating substances begin to form a clot to prevent blood loss. The immune system is alerted and begins to produce antitoxins to fight disease-producing organisms. All this very complex activity occurs without our being aware of what is happening within. Even if we are aware of what is happening, we still can't stop the process.

Psychological defense mechanisms are no different. They do not go into action at our direction. We are unaware of their operation, and, until gaining an awareness of them through recovery, an addict can do nothing to stop them. It is therefore futile as well as nonsensical to tell alcoholics or other people with addictions to "stop denying," "stop rationalizing," or "stop projecting," when they are not aware that they are doing so. They must first be helped to become aware of what they are doing.

During my internship, a patient I treated helped me understand the defensive nature of unconscious denial.

"That Just Couldn't Happen to Me"

The patient, a fifty-year-old woman, was admitted to the hospital for exploratory surgery because of a suspected tumor. She told the doctor that she was very active in community affairs and had assumed many important responsibilities. Although a tumor might mean cancer, it was important to her that she know the truth, since it would be unfair to many people and many organizations to continue carrying responsibilities if her health deteriorated. The doctor promised to be frank and reveal all the findings of surgery.

Surgery revealed that she did indeed have a cancerous tumor. Complying with her request for complete truthfulness, the doctor had a frank talk with the patient, telling her that the malignant tumor had to be removed for the cancer to be arrested. Furthermore, because the tumor showed some indications it had already spread, the patient would need to undergo chemotherapy.

Thanking the doctor for being truthful, she agreed to cooperate with whatever treatment was recommended. She spoke freely with the nurses and the staff about her cancer.

After being discharged from the hospital, she returned weekly for chemotherapy. She often remarked to hospital personnel how fortunate she was to be living in an era when science had provided a successful treatment for cancer. She appeared to be adjusting well, both physically and emotionally.

Five or six months after her surgery, however, she began to have various symptoms. The cancer had spread in spite of the chemotherapy. Eventually she developed severe joint pain and shortness of breath and was admitted to the hospital for further treatment. When I was doing the admission workup on her, she remarked, "I can't understand what is wrong with you doctors. I've been coming here regularly, and you just haven't been able to find out what's wrong with me."

The remark astonished me, since she had repeatedly referred to herself as having cancer. After thinking about it, I realized that as long as she saw cancer as some kind of abstract concept that did not pose an immediate threat to her life, she could accept the diagnosis. Once the condition began causing pain and shortness of breath, concrete evidence that she was deteriorating, she felt so threatened that her psychological system shut off realization of the truth. She was not intentionally lying nor pretending; she actually did not believe that she had cancer.

Denial as a Defense

Looking at denial as a defense, the obvious question is, A defense against what? In the case cited, the woman couldn't accept the devastating realization that she had a fatal disease and that her life may soon end.

In the case of an addicted person, what is so terrifying that the addict's psychological system opts to deny reality? The answer is that awareness of being an alcoholic or a drug addict is beyond acceptance. Why?

- The person may feel stigmatized at being labeled an alcoholic or addict.
- The person may consider addiction to indicate a personality weakness or moral degeneracy.
- The person may think not being able to use alcohol or other drugs again is frightening.

- The person may not accept the concept of being powerless and not in control.

It could be a combination of these and other reasons, but the addicted person finds accepting the diagnosis of addiction every bit as devastating as the woman did accepting the truth of her cancer. Until denial is overcome, addicts are not lying when they say they aren't dependent on chemicals. They are truly unaware of their dependency.

Rationalization and projection serve at least two main functions: (1) they reinforce denial, and (2) they preserve the status quo.

Rationalization

Rationalization means providing "good" reasons instead of the true reason. Like denial, this defense is not exclusive to chemically dependent people, though addicts can be very adept at it. Note that rationalization means offering good, that is, plausible reasons. This does not mean that all rationalizations are good reasons. Some are downright silly, but they can be made to sound reasonable. Rationalizations divert attention from true reasons. They not only divert others' attention from the truth, but also the addict's. As with denial, rationalization is an unconscious process—that is, the person is unaware of rationalizing.

A fairly reliable rule of thumb is that when people offer more than one reason for doing something, they are probably rationalizing. Usually the true reason for any action is a single one.

Because rationalizations sound reasonable, they are very deceptive, and anyone can get taken in by them.

A woman who graduated as an accountant was reluctant to apply for a promising job because she was afraid of being turned down. However, the reasons she gave her family were different: (1) they are probably looking for someone with years of experience; (2) the office is too far away to travel to every day; and (3) the starting wage is unsatisfactory.

A recovering alcoholic stopped going to AA. His reason? "I work in a rehabilitation center and I see alcoholics and addicts all day. I really don't need another hour of them at night." While his reason may seem plausible, the real reason for his avoiding AA was that he wished to drink again, and attending AA would make this difficult.

Rationalization reinforces denial. The alcoholic might say: "I am not an alcoholic. I drink because . . ." To the addict, an apparently valid reason for drinking means that he or she is not addicted.

Rationalizing also preserves the status quo, making the addict feel it is acceptable not to make necessary changes. This characteristic of addictive thinking can operate long after an addict overcomes denial and becomes abstinent. Brian's story is an example of how rationalization preserves the status quo.

Lost Love

Brian, a twenty-nine-year-old man, consulted me two years after he finished chemical dependency treatment. Although successfully staying abstinent, Brian was at an impasse. He had dropped out of college and was unsuccessful at holding a job. Brian typically did very well at work, but when his performance led to advancement or increased responsibility, he would leave the job.

Brian claimed to know exactly what his problem was. He was in love with Linda, and they had been engaged. Linda's parents, however, objected to the marriage and convinced her to break off the relationship.

Although this had happened more than five years before, Brian still loved Linda and hadn't gotten over the rejection. He was still grieving the loss, he said, and the thing that held him back was his continuing attachment to Linda.

As painful as romantic rejections may be, people do get over them eventually. Why was Brian different?

For several sessions, Brian and I tried to analyze the relationship to Linda and his reaction to the rejection. I proposed a variety of theories, all of which sounded logical, but both Brian and I felt that they didn't quite fit.

One night, after a session with Brian, I dreamed I was rowing a boat. As a child, I had especially liked boat rowing, but not being able to swim, I was not permitted to go out on a boat without an adult. So I would go to the pier where the boats were anchored, and, while the boat was securely tethered to the pier, I would row to my heart's content. There was little danger in doing this because the boat could not go anywhere. While I rowed I would fantasize getting to the other side of the lake and discovering a hitherto unknown land. I would plant the American flag on this new frontier just as some explorers had done. It was quite a normal fantasy for a ten-year-old boy.

When I awoke, Brian's situation became crystal clear to me. In my case, I was not being held back from my adventures by the tether to the pier. I *needed* that tether because it was my security.

Brian's situation was similar. For whatever reasons, he was terribly insecure. On one hand, going to college or accepting advancement at work might result in failure, and he did not want to take that risk. On the other hand, he could not accept that his stagnation was due to his apprehension, because that would mean admitting that he was not assertive or brave enough.

What Brian did was similar to what I had done with the boat. Just as I had tied myself to the pier, Brian had tied himself to an event in his life that he felt was holding him back. Because being rejected is painful and depressing, and because people often do lose motivation and initiative following a romantic rejection, this sounded perfectly reasonable to Brian and those around him. *Poor Brian. Isn't it a shame what happened to him? The poor boy cannot get over his unrequited love.*

Attributing his problem to Linda's rejection was a rationalization. It was a good explanation why Brian could not get on with his life, but *it was not the true reason.* Efforts at understanding why Brian's relationship prevented him from resolving his grief were futile because they were addressing the wrong point. Like other rationalizations, "the rejection by Linda" was a smoke screen.

The truth is that Brian did not want to deal with his insecurities and anxieties. Only after I refused to even hear of Linda, and instead focused on his need to cope with the challenge of getting on with his life, did Brian make the changes he had been avoiding.

Pain

Surprisingly, physical pain can be a type of rationalization. Not infrequently, we see people who are addicted to pain-killing medications who say they are unable to stop using the drugs because of severe pain. Often they have had one or more surgical procedures, and have become addicted to the drugs they took for persistent pain following surgery. People with this type of drug use do not think of themselves as addicts. "I never went out on the street to get high. I need the medication because the pain is unbearable. If I could get rid of the pain, I would not use drugs."

In these cases, examination by doctors usually fails to reveal a physical cause for the persistent pain, and these patients may be told, "You don't have real pain. It's all in your mind." They are often accused of pretending or malingering.

What is not generally recognized is that the unconscious mind can produce pain, real pain, that hurts as much as a fractured leg. Although some addicts feign pain in order to get the drugs they want, it is also possible for someone to have chronic pain that is not a put-on, but is nevertheless a product of the addiction.

People with this type of pain are, in a sense, rationalizing. Although they are not fabricating excuses, their unconscious mind is essentially doing it for them. Because their system craves drugs, the unconscious mind produces pain. All these people feel is pain, and they demand relief. Unfortunately, many doctors feel compelled to respond to their requests and continue prescribing medication.

Chronic pain addicts present a challenge to treatment, but many have been successfully treated. One young woman, who had a severe narcotic addiction because of persistent back pain, is now drug free. When asked how she now manages this pain without drugs, she responds, "What pain?"

Projection

Projection means placing the blame on others for things we are really responsible for ourselves. Like rationalization, projection serves two functions:

1. It reinforces denial.
   - "I am not an alcoholic. She makes me drink."
   - "If you had my boss, you'd use drugs too."
2. It helps preserve the status quo.
   - "Why should I make any changes? I'm not the one at fault. When others make the appropriate changes, I won't need to drink or use any other drug."

Blaming someone else seems to relieve an addict from the responsibility of making changes: "As long as you do this to me, you cannot expect me to change." Since the others are not likely to change, the drinking and other drug use can continue.

Trying to convince addicts that their arguments are not valid is usually unproductive. Since addictive projection primarily serves to sustain the use of chemicals, it will disappear on its own when sobriety is achieved. The best approach to take is to remind addicts, "You cannot change anyone but yourself. Let's work on bringing about the healthy changes in yourself that you can make."

Addicts, as well as others with psychological problems, may blame their parents for their shortcomings, something which pop psychology has inadvertently encouraged. Some addicts spend countless hours rehashing the past and tend to use such information to indulge in self-pity and to justify their recourse to chemicals. I have found it helpful to say, "Even if you are what your parents made you, if you stay that way, it's your own darn fault. We're not going to undo the past. Let's focus on making the necessary changes to improve your functioning."

These three major elements of addictive thinking—denial, rationalization, and projection—must be addressed at every stage of recovery. They may be present in layers, much like the layers of an onion. As one layer of denial, rationalization, and projection is peeled away, another is discovered underneath. The progressive elimination of these distortions of reality allows for improvement in recovery.

7

Dealing with Conflict

It has been said that the difference between psychosis and neurosis is that the psychotic says, "Two plus two equals five," while the neurotic says, "Two plus two equals four, and I can't stand it."

The nonaddict accepts that two plus two equals four and adjusts to this without too much difficulty. The addict, too, may adjust well at times. But at other times the chemical makes the addict psychotic, and at still other times neurotic. When reality seems too unbearable, the addict neither adjusts to it nor fantasizes it away. Rather, an actively practicing addict uses chemicals and becomes oblivious to reality.

With abstinence, an addicted person must face reality without the escape chemicals offer. This may help us understand why families of addicts, who may have long been demanding that the addict stop using chemicals, are sometimes disappointed when the addict finally stops. The abstinent addict who has not had help in overcoming addictive thinking may actually be harder to live with than a practicing addict. Some families have even nudged an addict into drinking or using again.

Contrary to common belief, addicts do not have more conflict in their lives than anyone else—that is, before chemical use messes everything up. Once the addiction is well under way, the chemically confused mind can generate a lot of conflict. Overwhelming conflict is not responsible for chemical dependency. Rather, it is the addict's distorted perception that makes reality unacceptable.

A Distorted Self-Image

The biggest distortion is in the addict's self-image. In one or more ways, the addict feels grossly inadequate.

- A drug-addicted young woman will not date or look at herself in the mirror because she believes she is ugly.
- A man who is chemically dependent and the author of a textbook on medical pathology is extremely anxious lecturing to physicians because he's afraid someone might disagree with him, although he is the acknowledged international authority.
- An alcoholic, a highly skilled attorney, lives in terror because she thinks what she is doing isn't good enough. "My life is like walking through a minefield," she says.

When the layers of veneer are peeled off, an addict has an extremely low self-esteem. If the distorted self-concept is not corrected, the addictive thinker will find it difficult or impossible to maintain recovery and could develop psychosis, neurosis, or a substitute addiction.

The misconception addicts have of themselves precedes the development of a chemical dependency, often by many years. The low self-esteem that comes with the use of chemicals is of a different kind—it is not related to a misconception about reality. There is nothing elevating about forgetting what happened yesterday, having a hangover, being a public spectacle, or waking up in jail. These are legitimate reasons why addicts might develop low self-esteem.

Changing a Negative Self-Image

Susan, a thirty-seven-year-old teacher, was admitted for treatment following a suicide attempt. She had just lost her job due to alcoholism. She had tried to conceal the alcohol on her breath by drinking vanilla extract, but her dysfunction progressed nevertheless, leading to her dismissal.

Susan was extremely depressed and very much down on herself. When I asked her to list some of her personality strengths, she could find no redeeming features in herself.

I then pointed out to Susan that she had graduated *summa cum laude* and had won the Phi Beta Kappa award. "The least you could have reported," I said, "is that you are intellectually bright. After all, they don't give such awards to stupid people."

Susan shook her head sadly. "When they told me that I'd won the Phi Beta Kappa award, I knew they'd made a mistake."

Changing the negative self-image of an addict, the low self-esteem that preceded chemical use, requires that the addict come to believe he or she really is an adequate person. This is a major challenge for someone whose life is in ruins. And we must remember that it is not only the low self-esteem of this "ruined" person that needs correction, but also even that of the pre-"ruined" person. Many addicts seek escape in chemicals because they feel they cannot cope. They must learn they do have healthy coping capabilities. The following story shows how, deep down, the ability to cope with conflict is already there.

Becoming Aware of What's Already There

Once as I sat down to pay my monthly bills, I was terribly upset to discover that I didn't have enough money in the checking account. I racked my brain to figure where the money had gone, but to no avail. I was left with the options of (1) taking out a loan or (2) letting bills go unpaid that month. Neither option was pleasant, but I chose the second.

About ten days later my bank statement arrived, and I was pleasantly surprised to discover there was more money in the bank account than I had thought. I had simply forgotten to record a deposit. There was no need for me to have been upset or to take out a loan.

My problem was that although I did have adequate funds to pay my bills, I was unaware of this. My perception of reality was incorrect. I had to become aware that I did not need a loan.

In the same way, addictive thinkers need to become aware of what is already there. They invariably have the ability to cope with conflicts, once they become aware that they have the skills they need.

How do we convince people with low self-esteem that they have self-worth? We begin by having that conviction about them. If we value them as worthy human beings, we can safely assume that our feelings will be conveyed to them. Empty compliments and flattery are of no value, but we must always be on the alert to identify every positive feature in their past and present, and give them reason to feel proud. Generally, people are quite adept at catching others doing something wrong. In dealing with addicts, we must be alert to "catch" them doing something right, and commend them for it.

With addicts, overcoming their misconception of reality is very complicated. Someone who is now, say, forty-two may have had self-doubts since the age of three. Much time and effort will be needed to undo that misconception. Remember, to the addict, this misconception is reality.

The Either / Or Rule

Addictive thinking is often also characterized by a rigidity of thought, what we may call "the either/or rule." The addicted person is likely to think in extremes, with little understanding that there is flexibility in resolution of problems.

For example, a newly recovering husband may not be able to decide whether to divorce or to stay with his wife. He could try a temporary separation while he begins to work on his sobriety and his wife gets counseling, but this alternative has probably never occurred to him.

This lack of flexibility or consideration of alternatives causes a lot of frustration, because most people are not comfortable with either extreme choice. It is not clear why other options and intermediate possibilities between extremes do not occur to an addictive thinker.

Still, the addict's logic does not appear faulty. If there were only the two choices, both unsatisfactory, frustration would be justified. If we were unaware of the nature of addictive thinking, we could get fooled by and share the addict's frustration when conflicts arise. Being alert to this should enable us to help the addict find appropriate solutions.

8

Hypersensitivity

To better understand the attitudes and reactions of the addict, it is important to know where this person is coming from. We can understand a person's extremely unusual reactions to a certain experience only if we understand the conditions surrounding the experience.

If we were to see someone reacting angrily to what appears to be hardly noticeable contact, say, brushing against someone in a crowded elevator, we would probably wonder, *What's wrong with that person?* Or we might think this person has a very short fuse. We would likely consider the angry reaction unwarranted.

Suppose, however, that the person involved had a blistering sunburn. The entire picture now changes. What appeared to be superficial contact was actually enough to elicit excruciating pain, and even if the angry outburst was not justified, at least we can understand why it occurred.

While a sunburn is apparent to everyone who can see, people's emotional sensitivities are not. We may therefore fail to understand an intense reaction if we are not aware of a person's peculiar sensitivities.

I have often wondered why some people resort to using alcohol and other drugs to feel better and others do not. Genetic and physiological differences in people play an important role in the development of addictions. But these are certainly not the entire answer.

Relief from Feelings of Distress and Discomfort

Though many people use alcohol and other drugs to get high, many others use chemicals just to feel normal. For these chemically dependent people, alcohol and other drugs are emotional anesthetics as they seek relief from feelings of distress and discomfort.

Certainly, just about everyone's life has plenty of stressful circumstances. But most people do not use alcohol or other drugs to cope with their distress.

Some people seem to have greater sensitivity to stress. These people apparently feel emotional discomfort more acutely than others. Many addicts are emotionally hypersensitive and are likely to have more intense emotions than nonaddicts. Chemically dependent people often seem to be almost inordinately sensitive with emotions of extreme intensity. When they love, they love intensely, and when they hate, they hate intensely.

The emotional sensitivity of the addict may be similar to the hypersensitive skin of a sunburn victim. A stimulus that might not produce emotional pain in a nonaddict can produce great distress in an addict.

Many addicts are loners. On the surface, they may seem to be antisocial and enjoy solitude, but that isn't necessarily true. Human beings by nature crave companionship. The loner doesn't really enjoy isolation, but sees it as the lesser of two evils. Mingling with people exposes the addict to the possibility of rejection. While rejection wouldn't be pleasant for anyone, to the addict it is devastating. The addict often anticipates rejection, where someone else may not even think of it.

Ironically, the anticipation of rejection may result in the torment of suspense, which may be so intolerable that the addict becomes abusive and provocative, provoking the rejection in order to be relieved of the suspense. At other times addicts seek to avoid rejection by being clinging and possessive. Social withdrawal, abusive behavior, and fanatic jealousy are thus often found among addicts.

Earlier, I mentioned that distorted, addictive logic is not always a consequence of chemical use, but often precedes it. The same is true of emotional hypersensitivity.

"I Didn't Belong with You-all"

A man in his nineteenth year of recovery said in an AA talk, "When I got to be about nine years old or so, I began to feel that I was different from you-all. I can't tell you why I felt different, but that is just the way I felt. If I walked into a room full of people, I felt I didn't belong with you-all, and that didn't feel good. I just didn't belong. Years later, when I took my first drink, I suddenly felt the world was right with me. I belonged."

This example vividly illustrates the intense feelings of being different that most addicts experience even before they use their first drug.

As sensitive as a sunburn may be, a sunburnt person knows that although someone's touch may elicit sharp pain, usually no offense was intended. Hypersensitive addicts, however, often aren't aware of their extreme emotional sensitivity, so they see hostile intent in innocent acts or remarks and are apt to react accordingly.

When we observe the reactions of a person using addictive logic, let's keep in mind the example of the sunburnt person. It may help us better understand.

9

Morbid Expectations

Frequently, addictive thinkers, for no logical reason, will feel apprehensive, anticipating disaster.

Good and bad things happen in this world. Most people experience both. Addicts are not the only people who worry and anticipate negative happenings, but they tend to do this more often than other people.

Some people are optimists. When they see a heap of manure, they look for a pony. Other people are pessimists. When they see a beautiful buffet laden with tempting food, they worry about food poisoning. Learning why people develop such opposing attitudes is not always easy.

Many addicted people are unable to see good in good happenings. Addictive thinkers seem burdened by a morbid feeling of being jinxed. On one hand, addictive thinkers fear that anything that appears to be working well will eventually fail. Some addicted people have a pattern of building to the verge of success and then sabotaging themselves.

Feelings of Impending Doom

Tom, age thirty-two, had never put together more than three months of abstinence. During his last rehab, however, he appeared to have turned the corner. Tom was approaching his first anniversary of sobriety, but three days before that significant date, he was admitted for detox.

Tom cried as he said, "You've got to believe me. I don't enjoy drinking. I'd never been dry for more than three months since

I was twelve, and now it was nearly a year. I was promoted at work, and for the first time in ages, my wife told me she loved me.

"I knew it was too good to last. I knew something terrible was about to happen. Each time the phone rang, I just knew it was to tell me that my little girl had been hit by a car. I drank to get the darn thing over with."

It is important to understand the morbid expectations of addictive thinking. Family and therapists may feel encouraged by the recovering person's success on the job and apparent happiness. There may be no telltale signs that beneath this superficial happiness, the recovering person is thinking, *I can't make it.* Sometimes this nagging anticipation becomes so unbearable that the addict thinks, *Oh, what the hell, I might as well get it over with,* and then precipitates the failure.

If the recovering person were using normal logic, it would be reasonable to reassure him or her that everything is going well and that there is no reason to expect sudden reversal. But if the recovering person is still operating out of addictive logic (which does not disappear immediately with abstinence), reasonable arguments will have no effect. The addict in early recovery may seem outwardly agreeable when these issues are discussed logically, but another thought system is operating inside.

When we discuss methods of helping an addicted person, we will address this problem. For now, let's just be aware that addicts often feel they are walking under a dark cloud of impending doom.

10

Manipulating Others

Addictive thinking may exist prior to the abuse of alcohol and other drugs. But there is one characteristic that appears to be generated by chemical addiction: manipulation.

Nonaddicts are occasionally manipulative, and addicts may have manipulated other people before they began to drink or use other drugs. But with the use of alcohol and other drugs, the problem escalates. People are forced into lying, covering up, and manipulating. Addicted people develop expertise at manipulating and, over time, this becomes an ingrained character trait.

Manipulation may start as a defensive maneuver to explain away the use of alcohol and other drugs, or to cover up problems, or to create situations that will facilitate drinking or using. But sooner or later it takes on a life of its own. The addict manipulates just to manipulate and lies just to lie, even though there may be nothing to gain. Manipulation and lying, instead of being a means to an end, actually become ends in themselves.

Avoiding Being Conned

During his using and drinking days, Phil would often come home at dawn or even disappear for days. After leaving rehab, Phil attended AA/NA meetings frequently. One night after a meeting, he and several friends went to an all-night coffee shop where they continued a mini-meeting until after midnight.

Phil's wife was terrified by his failure to return home at 10:30 as expected and assumed the worst. When Phil finally came in the door, she demanded, "Why didn't you call to let me know you were going to be late?"

"I did call," Phil said, "but there was no answer."

Phil's wife knew that the phone had not rung and was skeptical about his account of the coffee-bar mini-meeting. She was reassured only when Phil's sponsor verified the story.

I discussed the incident with Phil, and he said, "I don't know why I told her I had called. I knew it was a lie, but it just seemed natural for me to do."

I often caution people entering treatment that they must be careful not to con themselves. People might gain a temporary advantage by putting something over on others, but it's a hollow triumph when they con themselves. The victor is also the vanquished.

Early in recovery, some addicts claim to have a flash of insight. It suddenly strikes them how blind they have been to their addiction, and how selfish and inconsiderate they have been.

They may think, *I am certainly not stupid enough to revert back to my destructive behavior now that I have become aware of it.*

Having had this vision of truth, they may elect to leave treatment because they "no longer need it." Or, if they do remain in treatment, they may become "therapists" for other patients, helping them to achieve a similar flash of insight.

Nonsense! Years of addictive thinking and behavior do not melt away overnight. In spite of addicts' protests of sincerity, they are manipulating. The tragedy is that addicts have conned themselves into believing they have achieved instant recovery.

An unwary therapist may be taken in by the addict's sudden insight. How wonderful not to have to laboriously chisel away at the mountain of denial as with other clients! What a relief to have someone who can promptly begin working on the important issues of recovery! Here is someone who is ready to do a Fourth Step (taking a moral inventory) in the second week of treatment, and a Fifth Step (sharing his or her life history with another person) on the very next day!

This is a person who takes a high-speed elevator rather than the Twelve Steps. The therapist needs to beware. This is pure manipulation. Odds are that this person will stop at the nearest bar on the way home from the treatment center.

A shortcut is often the quickest way to some place you weren't going. Why would someone take such a shortcut? Because in contrast to normal thinking, where people may use shortcuts to reach a goal faster, in addictive thinking the shortcut is the goal. It doesn't have to go anywhere in particular.

As with other aspects of addictive thinking, the addict's shortcuts and manipulations do not appear to be obviously absurd, and it is easy to get taken in. Furthermore, these manipulations do not disappear immediately with abstinence from chemicals. Much time must elapse and much work must be done before the recovering addict can overcome manipulative behavior.

11

Guilt and Shame

It is commonly thought that addicts are guilt-ridden. Certainly when we hear an addicted person express remorse, we sense how deeply guilty this person feels.

Addicts may indeed feel genuine remorse, but often they feel not guilt but shame. There is a big difference.

The Difference between Guilt and Shame

The main distinction between guilt and shame is this:

- The guilty person says, "I feel guilty for something I have done."
- The shame-filled person says, "I feel shame for what I am."

Why is the distinction so important? Because people can apologize, make restitution, make amends, and ask forgiveness for what they have *done;* they can do pathetically little about what they *are.* Alchemists during medieval times spent their working lives futilely trying to convert lead into gold. A person feeling shame doesn't even try, thinking, *I cannot change my substance. If I'm made up of inferior material, there is no reason for me to make any effort to change myself. It would be an act of futility.*

Guilt can lead to corrective action. Shame leads to resignation and despair.

Close analysis of addicted people often reveals very low self-esteem and deep-seated feelings of inferiority.

How Shame Develops

It is not always possible to discover how feelings of shame developed. Shame can be the result of many things: The book *Letting Go of Shame* by Ronald and Patricia Potter-Efron lists genetic and biochemical makeup, culture, family, shaming relationships, and self-shaming thoughts and behavior as sources of shame.* But another major contributing factor may be the way human beings come into the world. Humans are helpless and remain dependent longer than any other living being. Animal cubs run around when they are just days old, and weeks after birth many forage for their own food. Humans would die without adult care for the first several years of life. And even if they are physically self-sufficient, some children remain economically dependent on parents well into the third decade of life. Being dependent on others does not foster self-esteem. Helplessness and dependency can generate feelings of inferiority.

It takes enlightened effort by parents to help their children develop self-esteem. Parents who are overprotective or do too much for children do not allow them to develop a sense of mastery. Parents who make demands on children when they are not yet capable of fulfilling them can cause children to feel inadequate. Ideal parental and environmental circumstances are rare; thus, many people grow up with shaky self-esteem.

Why Addicts Feel Shame

The feeling of low self-esteem or shame in addicts is usually more severe. Circumstances that ordinarily cause feelings of guilt in emotionally healthy people bring feelings of shame to

* Ronald and Patricia Potter-Efron, *Letting Go of Shame: Understanding How Shame Affects Your Life* (Center City, Minn.: Hazelden Educational Materials, 1989), 2.

addicts as a kind of short circuit. Suppose you flip the switch for the air conditioner, but instead the lights go on; or you turn on the dishwasher and the garbage disposal starts up. Obviously the wires are crossed. That is what happens with addicts. What should produce guilt instead produces shame.

Because addictive behavior often results in improper, irresponsible, and even immoral actions, there is ample reason for the addict to develop much guilt. Instead, the addict develops profound shame.

Shame is not only unproductive but also counterproductive. Suppose you had an automobile that was operating well, but a part became defective. You would replace the defective part, and the car would run well again. If, however, you found your car was a lemon and each time you corrected a problem something else went wrong, you might throw your hands up in disgust. You might justifiably conclude there is no purpose in getting the car repaired.

This is what happens in addictive thinking. The profound shame that addicts feel results in their thinking that it is futile to change their ways. Guilt might have been undone by making amends, but amends cannot change the defective material addicts feel they are made of.

Remorse in the addict is as common as dandelions in the spring. The addict's tears can be heartrending. Any listener unaware of addictive thinking would swear that this person will never again touch another drop of liquor or take another drug.

Ed, a forty-four-year-old electrician, came to the rehab center from another city because he was afraid his alcoholism would be exposed by local treatment.

On admission, Ed was deep in remorse. "How could I have brought such disgrace to the people I love most? How could I have done that to my family? I love them and I've treated them badly. I'll kill myself before I ever take another drink."

Late that night the nurse called me to say that Ed was acting strangely. On my suggestion, she searched his room and found a bottle of vodka three-quarters empty.

Ed's remorse was not insincere, but it represented shame rather than guilt. Ed felt that no matter what he did, he would always be an inadequate husband and father, and being sober would not make him into a better person. The pain and the harm he had done to his family called for relief, and, since he felt it would make no difference whether or not he drank, he reverted to the vodka that he had smuggled into the facility where he planned to get sober. That is addictive thinking.

Psychologist and addictions specialist Rokelle Lerner says that the Twelve Step program changes shame into guilt. The program helps addicts understand that they have a disease. While addicts are held fully responsible for their behavior, they are not at fault for having that disease. Addicts are expected to follow their treatment program and be totally abstinent, however, as well as make major changes in their character traits.

As addicts find acceptance among other recovering people and discover that people who have adhered to the program and made substantial changes in their character are respected and loved, they begin to realize that they, too, may be basically a good person. What is necessary is abstinence and a personality overhaul. This is how shame changes into guilt. Doing a personal inventory, sharing it with another person, and beginning to make amends all help to abate guilt. Addicts who work these Steps become constructive persons and begin to receive the love and respect of their families and community.

12

Omnipotence and Impotence

One feature of addictive thinking is the illusion of being in control. To some degree, a delusion of omnipotence (feeling one has unlimited power) is present in every addict and codependent.

Most people addicted to alcohol or other drugs eventually lose control over the chemical; yet they insist they can control it. Although their lives have become grossly unmanageable, they steadfastly insist they are still in charge. This inability to admit loss of control in defiance of reality is characteristic of addictive thinking. It is a delusion of omnipotence and must be overcome before a recovering person can admit and accept powerlessness, a required First Step in recovery.

Illusions of Control

Alcoholics may have many excuses why Alcoholics Anonymous is not for them. They may object, "I've been to AA meetings. They talk about God all the time, and I'm an atheist. I don't believe in God, so I can't use AA."

The problem, however, isn't that the addict doesn't believe there is a God. Most believe deep down that there is. The problem is, they think they're God.

There are many things over which a person has no control or is powerless. This does not in anyway constitute a character weakness. Hay-fever sufferers can't control whether or not they sneeze. They may obtain relief by proper medical treatment, but without it, they are powerless over sneezing. Yet, even the worst sneezing attack doesn't make hay-fever sufferers feel like second-class citizens. To insist that they control their sneezing, when in fact they can't, would be delusional.

People who think of addiction as a moral failure, rather than as a disease, see failure to control drinking or using drugs as a character weakness. When people defensively deny their powerlessness over chemicals and insist they are in control, they are in fact being delusional. Any addict who says, "I cannot be powerless," is having a delusion of omnipotence.

AA is simply saying that because addicts have no control over their chemical use, they must obtain controls from elsewhere. It is this "elsewhere" that constitutes a Higher Power. Someone who does not believe in a religious Higher Power may find other external sources of control. Many, for example, consider their AA group to be a Higher Power.

In order to accept a Higher Power, whether it be religious or otherwise, addicts must realize that they are not in control of some aspect of life. Indeed, this is what hay-fever sufferers do when they take a (nonaddictive) medication.

Delusions of Grandeur

Along with the delusion of omnipotence, addicts have an attitude and a fantasy of grandiosity, another feature of addictive thinking. Grandiosity in addictive thinking exists in stark defiance of reality, as the following story illustrates.

The "CEO" with No Keys

Mel, at one time a very successful business executive, suffered the all-too-familiar loss of family, business, and home. Sitting at the bar, he would cry into his beer, fantasizing that at any moment someone would walk in and offer him the position as chief executive officer of a major corporation.

This man eventually entered rehabilitation, and during his

entire stay, he was full of grandiosity. Certain he was better than anyone else, he looked down his nose at everyone. He objected to the recommendation that after treatment he go to a halfway house, even though he had nowhere else to go. Grudgingly and condescendingly he went to the halfway house, still grandiose. Reality notwithstanding, he continued to believe he was still the successful executive.

The moment of truth came after six weeks in the halfway house. Mel recalls it this way: "I was standing outdoors, with my hands in my pockets. Removing the contents of my right pocket, I found I had twelve cents and a trouser button. Then I felt in my left pocket, and it suddenly hit me that I had no keys. I didn't own anything I needed a key for! No apartment, no office, no car." Not until this point did he accept reality.

Grandiosity and the delusion of omnipotence often go together. Both may well be desperate efforts to avoid the awareness of impotence.

Human beings are, after all, impotent in many ways. Many things in life—the weather, other people, the price of milk—are beyond our control. Many parts of us, both physically and psychologically, are beyond our control.

People who feel good about themselves are not usually threatened by an awareness of their impotence. But when people have no self-esteem—when they feel inadequate, incompetent, and worthless—they must protect themselves against what they see as another put-down: the inability to control chemicals. Building self-esteem can help recovering addicts overcome this subtle yet powerful threat.

13

Admitting Errors

Many chemically dependent people have great difficulty admitting they are wrong. They may disagree with this statement, asserting that they would not have the slightest difficulty admitting they were wrong, *if* that were ever to occur.

One of the features of addictive thinking is the addict's perception of always being right. Many of the other traits prevalent in addictive thinking—denial, projection, rationalization, omnipotence—are brought into play to bolster the insistence that the person has always been right.

Being Human Means Making Errors

The way addicts explain and defend their behavior may sound perfectly logical. Each explanation may at first seem reasonable. Taking the entire litany of incidents and explanations into account, however, we must ask, "If the addict were indeed error-free, how did things end up in such a horrible mess?" After we reexamine the addict's account, the addictive thinking becomes evident. Addicts' logical-sounding explanations are often only ingenious rationalizations and projections.

The recovering person must learn not only that it is all right to be human, but also that it is the greatest achievement of all to be a fine human being. But one must first be human, which means that one must err at some time or another.

One of the most effective ways to accept the statement, "Making a mistake is not the end of the world," is seeing other people, especially those an addict holds in high regard, make mistakes too. Anyone can serve as a model for this. An example comes from my own life.

Ill-Fated Reunion

I once had a young psychiatric patient who was hospitalized for an extended time. As he recovered, he was given passes to leave the hospital for several hours.

One Friday, the patient told me he wanted to attend a class reunion the next day and meet with his classmates before they left for the four corners of the earth. I saw no reason to deny this request. Before I left him, the patient said, "Please remember to write that pass order on the chart; otherwise, the nurses will not let me out." Promising to do so, I promptly went to the nurses' station and wrote the order.

When I met the patient the following Monday, he greeted me with a tearful and angry outburst. "Why did you lie to me? Why did you tell me I could go and then not let me go? Some of these classmates are going away, and I will never see them again!"

I told the patient that I had no idea what he was talking about, because I had written the pass order as I had promised.

"Then your nurses lied to me," he cried. "They said there was no such order on the chart."

I then examined the patient's chart, and, much to my amazement, there was no order there. What had happened to the order I remembered writing?

The mystery was solved when I subsequently discovered the order *on another patient's chart.* I had indeed written the order as I had promised, but the nurses were correct in telling the patient there was no order for a pass on his chart, as indeed there was not. It was on someone else's chart.

I took both charts to the patient's room and showed him what had happened. I apologized for my mistake that had deprived him of seeing his classmates, and I told him that there was nothing I could do to right this error. All I could do was apologize.

Something strange happened: After this incident, there was a significant and progressive improvement in this patient's condition. It later turned out that one of the patient's major hang-ups was perfectionism. Making a mistake was taboo. He was obsessed with perfectionism and terrified of making a mistake.

But look here! His doctor made a mistake! And it was not just *any* kind of mistake. A pass order written on the wrong chart could have conceivably resulted in a high-risk suicidal patient being permitted to leave the hospital. A doctor's mistake can be fatal, yet the doctor admitted it. Furthermore, the doctor continued to function as a doctor, the nurses still respected him, and his orders were still being followed, even though he had made a mistake! Ergo, mistakes do not demolish a person. Maybe he, the patient, didn't have to be eternally on guard to avoid a mistake.

Prompt Admission of Mistakes

When I first became familiar with the Twelve Step program, I was delighted to discover Step Ten, "And when wrong, promptly admitted it." Like many other people, I used to defend my mistakes. My ego would not allow me to admit I was wrong.

Some people will put up a vigorous battle to prove they were right, and only when all their arguments are rebutted will they grudgingly concede that they were wrong. This attitude can have disastrous consequences. It is a far simpler and a highly effective method of conserving one's energies to simply admit that one was wrong and to do it promptly without futile attempts at defending a mistake.

What a relief it has been to be free of this burden! I am not immune to making mistakes, and, when I admit my humanity, people invariably understand. It is only when I insist that I was right that I provoke their anger.

As one surrenders the delusion of omnipotence, which is part of addictive thinking, one is then able to admit one's errors.

14

Anger

Anger is a powerful and important emotion. Its management may well be the most difficult psychological problem of our era. While addiction literature has some fine books on anger management, we still need to understand more about the real essence of anger.

Three Phases of Anger

Anger may be subdivided into three phases. Phase 1 is the feeling of anger when provoked. If someone offends or hurts me, I feel angry. This is essentially an instinctive or *reflex* emotion, over which one has little control.

Phase 2 is the *reaction* to anger. When offended, I may bite my lips and say nothing, I may make a remark, I may hurl an expletive, or I may push or strike out. Although I may have no control over the feeling of anger, I have much control over my reaction.

Phase 3 is the *retention* of anger. Granted that I have no control over the initial feeling when provoked, but how long do I hang onto it? Minutes? A month? Fifteen years?

For convenience, let's refer to phase 1 as "anger," phase 2 as "rage," and phase 3 as "resentment."

Too often anger leads quickly to rage. Addicts seem to have particular difficulty with reacting to anger, even when not under the influence of a chemical. Of course, when self-control has been weakened by chemicals, the rage reaction may be very severe. Is there some way of diminishing the intensity of phase 1 anger?

All emotions have a function. Although religionists and secularists disagree on many issues, they do agree that everything in nature has a function. For example, the vast array of colors in the animal world, from the multicolored birds to the splendor of aquatic life, all serve some purpose. Colors may allow a creature to blend into the environment, serving as camouflage for protection. Or bright colors may help attract a mate.

We might ask, "What function does anger serve in nature?" It does not seem necessary for survival. If I were attacked, I might be able to defend myself adequately without becoming angry. Fear can exist without anger and can initiate the flight or fight reaction necessary for survival. Even without anger, I could recall who attacked me and be alert to possible future attacks.

Anger is not the same as hatred. We can be very angry at someone we love, and we can hate something without being angry at it. Then what purpose does anger serve?

I believe the natural purpose of anger is to preserve social order. Our feelings of outrage at someone being robbed, beaten, or harmed prompt us to take action to prevent such happenings. Without anger, we might defend ourselves adequately, but we might not make the effort to protect anyone else. Anger is an emotion evoked by injustice, toward ourselves or others.

But what is unjust? That depends on a person's thoughts, values, and beliefs. People differ sharply on what is just or unjust in this world. Thus, some people become angry much quicker than others.

Addicts and Intense Anger

Many addicts seem to think that the world is unfair to them. They feel victimized by everyone, and they are angry at everyone, including God. *Why me? Why are You doing this to me?*

The sensitivity of the addict to any perceived injustice is much like the sensitivity of a person with a migraine headache who may feel excruciating pain at bright lights or loud noises. Addicts often feel offended, belittled, and humiliated by everyone. Their families don't love them enough, their friends don't value their companionship enough, they don't get enough recognition from employers for their hard work, and so on. How much is enough? Given the hypersensitivity and the insatiable needs of some people, infinity may not be enough.

The problem, then, for addictive thinkers is not only in the severity of their rage reaction, but also in the distortion of their perceptions. For example, a man comes home from work and announces, "Hi, everybody, I'm home!" The wife and children, absorbed in an exciting television program, respond absent-mindedly and do not jump up to greet him. To this man, their lack of response indicates how little they value him. *How do you like that? I break my neck all day to provide adequately for them, and this is how they appreciate me.* To him, this lack of appreciation is a gross injustice, and he feels intense anger. Or, when his wife shows attention to her friends, he may feel she doesn't value him enough, and he becomes angry with her for "humiliating" him.

We can thus understand, although we don't excuse, the reactions of the addict who feels victimized by "injustice." Every culture accepts that perpetrators of injustices should be punished. That is what an addict who acts out anger is doing, punishing another for an "injustice." While techniques for managing anger are important, getting rid of the distorted thinking that generates the anger would obviously be most helpful.

How Recovery Helps

In recovery, an addict's perceptions undergo a gradual change. With the help of counseling and working the Twelve Step program, addicts become less self-centered and less exquisitely sensitive. As sobriety progresses, self-esteem improves and they no longer interpret everything as personal, as belittling. They begin to take responsibility for their actions and stop blaming others. Things that used to provoke anger and rage no longer do so.

This is much different from repression of anger. Repression occurs when there has been a true injustice, and when a person who has legitimate reason for feeling anger does not feel it at all. This is as abnormal as not feeling pain when stung by a sharp object. Certain people have learned, in one way or another, not to feel anger. This repression of anger is not a control technique whereby a person recognizes anger and decides to handle it in a certain way, such as slowly counting to ten. Repression is an unconscious psychological mechanism that keeps a person from being aware of an unacceptable emotion or idea. At an unconscious level of the mind, the anger may be felt, but it doesn't appear in the person's awareness.

"Feeling Anger Would Be Sinful"

A good example of repressed anger is a patient I treated for chronic depression. A nun with strict religious training, she had developed the idea that feeling anger is sinful.

To get to my office, Sister had to travel an hour and a half, taking two buses. She wanted to avoid being late for her appointment, but the bus schedule was such that she arrived about an hour early. I tried to always be prompt, and she always waited patiently.

One time I had to unexpectedly leave town, and I neglected to tell my secretary to call Sister and cancel the appointment. I later learned that after waiting long beyond her appointment time, Sister asked about the delay and was told that I was not in the office that day.

On my return I called Sister, apologized, and set another appointment. When she came to my office, I again expressed my regret for failing to notify her of this cancellation in advance.

"I'm sure that when you found out I was not in, you were very angry," I said.

Sister smiled. "No. Why should I be angry?"

"Because you traveled for an hour and a half and then waited two more hours, and you wasted a great deal of time because I neglected to call you. There is no way you could not have been angry."

Sister continued to smile sweetly. "I understand that these things can happen. You are a very busy man. I have no reason to be angry."

"I'll do my own apologizing," I replied. "I appreciate your consideration and your willingness to overlook my mistake, but don't tell me you did not feel offended."

With the same sweet, smiling expression, Sister said, "No, why should I feel offended?"

I am certain Sister was telling the truth when she said she did not feel offended and did not feel angry. Feeling is a sensation, and her sensory system did not register anger. It had been trained that way.

I think something is wrong with that. It's like discovering numerous burn marks on your hands and not recalling being burned. If your nervous system is intact, a burn should produce pain. If it does not, then something is wrong.

Voluntarily controlling one's reaction to anger is not wrong. Certainly it is not necessary to throw things, to hit the wall, or to shout obscenities. In fact, those who say a person should discharge anger by screaming or even hitting a punching bag have little clinical grounds for this recommendation. It is perfectly safe to decide not to manifest anger. But not to *feel* anger is something else. Not feeling anger indicates an unconscious denial and repression of anger, and this can cause problems. Little wonder that Sister was chronically depressed and suffering from high blood pressure and ulcers. Anger that is denied and repressed may result in depression and various physical diseases.

Men Do and Should Cry

When they have been hurt, many men become enraged, rather than offended. It seems that they should be crying, but instead they explode with anger. Perhaps this is because the normal reaction of crying is not available to them. Why? Because they believe "men don't cry." Many cultures equate masculinity with stoicism. For example, the newspapers may report that at a tragic incident, a man wept "unashamedly." Why should a man ever be ashamed of crying when hurt?

When deprived of the outlet of crying, the male psyche may seek another outlet, and this often results in rage. In fact, being deprived of the chance to cry when hurt is unjust, and perhaps this injustice converts the pain into anger and rage.

Upon entering recovery some men cry for the first time since their infancy. They learn that it is okay to feel; and, thus, one important source of anger is eliminated.

Getting Rid of Resentments

Phase 3, resentment, is managed especially well in the Twelve Step program. Recovering people are told, "If you hang on to resentments, you'll drink again." People at meetings unburden themselves of the grudges they have been harboring. In the process of doing so, they often become aware that they were misinterpreting another person's actions and that there is really no reason to hold a grudge. Sometimes, we may realize that what we thought was harmful to us was actually a blessing in disguise. Or we may realize the common sense of the idea that harboring a resentment is letting someone you don't like live inside your head rent free. Sharing perceptions and feelings with others and getting an objective perspective diminish resentments and may eliminate them altogether. The recovery program recognizes the destructive nature of rage and resentments.

People are not apt to consider being an addict highly desirable. But if we realize that the gains from recovery in a Twelve Step program may not be easily found in other ways, being addicted may not be the curse that we thought it to be.

15

The Confining Wall

Given the emotional sensitivity, poor self-image, and morbid expectations of addicts, it is understandable why they may try to protect themselves from anticipated discomfort. Addicts expect to be put down, criticized, or rejected. To defend their psyche against the pain that this causes, many addicts build a protective wall between themselves and the rest of the world.

Many addicts are self-described loners. Indeed, the only way they can associate with others without discomfort is when they have anesthetized themselves with chemicals. When not under the influence, they may withdraw passively or keep people at a distance by being self-righteous, hypercritical, or obnoxious.

The Porcupine Index

Although isolation spares the addicts from the anticipated discomfort inherent in associating with others, it also deprives them of the companionship that they crave. We might say that the addict is in a dilemma because of a high "porcupine index." The addict is like a porcupine who wishes to be in contact with other porcupines but fears that their quills will sting. Coming too close is painful, but keeping too distant is lonely. The porcupine must therefore carefully calculate how close to approach to achieve some companionship while avoiding being hurt.

While the defensive walls that addicts build protect them from the "stings" of the outside world, they are also very confining, frustrating the intense human craving for friendship. The wall that was built for protection thus turns out to be a prison.

Much of the addict's behavior reinforces the isolation. The lying, disappointing, manipulating, resenting, and criticizing behavior causes other people to shun him or her. The anger, self-centeredness, inconsideration, and irresponsibility make the addict's company undesirable. Although addicts act in ways that make other people avoid them, they nevertheless resent the isolation that results. Loneliness becomes more grist for the mill, another reinforcer of their poor self-image, and addicts try to escape by increasing the use of anesthetizing chemicals, perpetuating a vicious circle.

Shutting Out Family and Friends

Addicts' withdrawal from outside social contacts is bad enough, but the problem is aggravated when they build a defensive wall at home. Addicts often find that physical withdrawal is not easily achieved, and so behavioral tactics become the only available defense. This often results in abusive behavior toward those the addict loves most: spouse, children, parents, and siblings.

Initially, the addict's expectations of rejection are based on a misperception and become a self-fulfilling prophecy. Because addicts think so poorly of themselves, they think other people will reject them. As the defensive maneuvers increase, the anticipated rejection is no longer a fantasy. People do avoid them, which in turn reinforces their poor self-image.

If family or friends try to reach a loved one by breaking through the defensive wall or going around it, the addict may panic and reinforce the wall. For example, a woman requested treatment for drug addiction because she had used up all accessible veins in her body. Her appearance on admission to the rehab center was dreadful. When she appeared significantly healthier three weeks later, I remarked, "Celia, you're beginning to look good." My comment was greeted by an odious expletive.

The following day Celia came to my office to apologize for her insulting remark. "You don't understand," she said. "You said something positive to me. I don't know how to handle that." The initial treatment had at least made her aware of her provocative behavior, but it was months before she could accept a positive statement without discomfort. Without treatment she would have continued to repel anyone who reached out to her.

The Value of Support Groups

We can now understand both the necessity and the effectiveness of the anonymous fellowships. Associating with others who share the same problem is far less threatening than dealing with society as a whole. In support groups, addicts do not have to fear that they will be rejected. They discover that not only are there many respectable people who were at one time active addicts like themselves, but also that many people share their emotions and some of their character traits. They begin to better understand the defensive nature of addictive behaviors as they see them in others and learn to identify them in themselves. In the safe confines of fellowship meetings, addicts can begin to dismantle the defensive wall. At first, they take down the part of the wall that has kept out family and friends. Gradually, they begin to let in society as a whole.

The characteristics of addictive thinking are the tools the addict uses both in erecting the defensive wall and in maintaining it. With proper treatment, the vicious circle is interrupted; and, as misperceptions are corrected in recovery, the entire wall can eventually be eliminated.

16

Managing Feelings

Addicts may have great difficulty with their feelings. Negative feelings such as anger, envy, guilt, and hate are not the only ones difficult to manage. Even some positive feelings—for example, love, admiration, and pride—may baffle the addicted person, sometimes even more so after stopping chemical use.

Emotions are motivating forces; by definition, they are what make us move. They are like the automobile engine, which propels the car.

Think of a situation in which a driver is afraid of operating the vehicle. Perhaps this driver is behind the wheel of a racing car that generates such power and high speeds that the driver can't maintain control. Or perhaps the driver believes the brakes are failing or the steering mechanism is malfunctioning. Whatever the case, the driver will be very reluctant to sit behind the wheel, fearing loss of control and an accident.

When people fear their emotions, two things may be happening:

1. their emotions are so intense as to feel uncontrollable, or
2. they feel incapable of managing emotions of normal intensity. They doubt the reliability of their "brakes" and "steering mechanism."

While some chemically dependent people use alcohol or other drugs to get high, others use chemicals to feel normal. Mood-altering drugs are essentially emotional anesthetics: They numb feelings. When people stop using chemicals, those emotions that were primarily numbed by the chemical are going to be keenly felt.

Depression

Depression is one of the painful feelings that the addict may have anesthetized with alcohol and other drugs. It is little wonder that a newly abstinent person is apt to feel depressed. Abstinence unmasks previous feelings of depression. And the clarity of mind that follows abstinence allows the person to see the havoc that alcohol or other drug use has wrought on family, job, financial status, and physical health.

The "Joy" of a Cigarette Burn

Emily, a young woman of twenty-three, was admitted to the treatment center after eight years of using alcohol, pain pills, sedatives, and amphetamines. On the day following admission, she encountered me walking down the corridor and asked to have a few moments alone with me. She then fell on my shoulder and began crying bitterly. "I can't take it, Doc! I can't take it! It hurts so bad. I never felt pain like this before. Please help me, Doc! Give me something. I can't take the way I feel."

After she calmed down, I told her about a woman who, in an automobile accident, severed nerves that carry sensations from the upper right arm to the brain. Surgeons tried to repair the nerves. During the weeks of convalescence, her right arm hung limp with no feeling, lifeless as a sack of cement. Depressed and discouraged, she thought she would never have use of her right arm again.

One day someone dropped a lit cigarette on her right hand, and she felt the pain of the burn. She jumped up and ecstatically screamed, "I can feel! I can feel! It hurts! I can feel!" To anyone else, the pain would probably have been unpleasant. To this woman, pain was a joy because it indicated that her ability to feel was returning.

I told Emily that since age fifteen she had been living as a zombie, anesthetized with alcohol or other drugs and unable to feel any emotion. True, she had not felt much pain, but she couldn't have experienced many pleasant sensations either. Now that she was off drugs, she could feel the pain and joy of life again.

Newly recovering addicts may experience anxiety and panic when confronted with new feelings they have never learned to manage. They may believe being angry means feeling homicidal, loving means engulfing someone, being loved means being engulfed by someone, hating someone means alienating the whole world, and so on. Confronting these feelings is a formidable challenge.

Some people in early recovery fear having no control over a specific feeling. Not knowing how to isolate a particular feeling or manage it, they just shut off their whole feeling apparatus.

Emergence of Emotions

A newly abstinent addict is now subject to many feelings that had been anesthetized with chemicals. The initial reaction may be a kind of "numbness," similar to turning off the master valve, feeling nothing. In these cases, family members may be concerned that their loved one has become a "zombie." Other addicts may begin to express themselves in a manner their families and friends have never seen before, which may be frightening. Learning how to handle emotions takes time, and, if family members are uncomfortable with the newly recovering person's behavior, they may feel that the addict was actually easier to live with before sobriety. Sometimes family members may give the addict subtle cues that result in relapse.

It is therefore extremely important that both the addict and family members understand that in addiction feelings were the prime target of the chemicals, and that abstinence can initially result in an emotional chaos or emotional paralysis. Learning to evaluate and manage feelings is a major task. This will take time, with many trials and errors. The recovering person must have a great deal of patience, and those around this person may need it even more.

17

Flavors and Colors of Reality

Frequently, even when seeing reality accurately, an addict will feel that reality is just not good enough. The normal rewards and pleasures of life are just not enough. Something is missing, and the addict feels cheated out of the true pleasures. Other people who appear to be content must be experiencing the "real" thing, but somehow, the addictive thinker feels deprived of this. *There must be more to life,* the addict thinks.

From Gray to Rosy

Clancy, a popular AA speaker, says it so well: "My world was drab and gray. My family, my job, my home life, my car—all were gray. I cannot stand everything being gray. I need color! And alcohol provided color to life." To the alcoholic or other addict, life is like food cooked without seasoning: tasteless and unpalatable.

A sensory experience is personal and subjective. It is almost impossible to communicate your sensory experience to another person or to quantify it objectively. If two people taste the same dish, hear the same melody, or see the same sunset, there is no way that one can know exactly what the other is feeling.

Similarly, when nonaddicts try to understand the addict's use of chemicals, they may be at a loss. *What in heaven's name is wrong with this person who has a fine home, a good marriage, healthy children, and a rewarding job?* they ask themselves. *Why the dissatisfaction? Why does this person drink so much?* The answers may not be easy to accept.

- Why does this person drink so much? Alcoholics drink because they have the disease of alcoholism. They have lost control over their drinking due to this disease.
- Why the dissatisfaction? An addictive thinker's outlook on reality is distorted. Being chronically dissatisfied, addictive thinkers do not feel they are experiencing what they should experience. Life is not providing enough gratification, and alcohol or other chemicals seem to bring color to it all. The grays seem to change into dazzling colors. Now they feel what others must be experiencing in life. They feel normal.

When the chemical is taken from the addict, the addict faces symptoms of withdrawal. After these pass, the doldrums set in. The world seems gray again, devoid of color, of interest, of excitement, and of pleasure. Addicts entering recovery must realize that abstaining from chemicals will not be enough to make everything rosy.

How Clinical Depression and Addictive Depression Differ

If the addict should consult a psychiatrist, the addict's symptoms may appear similar to those of a depressed person suffering from a major affective (emotional) disorder:

- loss of interest in life
- inability to concentrate
- a feeling of futility
- a low sex drive and
- a feeling that life isn't worth living

Little wonder that psychiatrists often diagnose the condition as a major affective disorder or clinical depression, and prescribe antidepressant medication. For newly recovering addicts who do not have a clinical depression, these medications are notoriously ineffective and can be threatening to sobriety.

While the symptoms of the recovering addict and the person with a clinical depression can be similar, there are important differences.

A major *affective disorder* is essentially a biochemical disease. In other words, something has gone awry with the neurohormones, the chemicals that relay messages among the brain cells. The biochemical changes may be the result of severe stress to the system or may be due to genetic factors. The symptoms of a clinical depression have a fairly well-defined beginning. The person previously enjoyed life, was active, and had interests until some particular time when things began to change. Sometimes the change can be related to a physical event such as childbirth, menopause, surgery, or a severe virus. Other times it can be tied to an emotional incident such as a financial reversal, death of a loved one, or, strangely enough, a promotion at work. The important point is that the change in the person's feelings and attitudes can be traced to a starting point, perhaps several weeks or several months ago.

With *addiction,* the "depressive" symptoms often do not appear to have even an approximate beginning. Many times the person always felt that way, even as an adolescent. Addicts are likely to say they never believed they had a fair shake and that everyone else always had more or better things. They may have been thought of as thrill-seekers or hell-raisers. More often than not, addicts will say they had been dissatisfied with life for as long as they can remember.

This kind of depression is not relieved by antidepressant medications. All they are likely to do is produce annoying side effects. Although tricyclic antidepressants and monoamine oxidase inhibitors (MAOI antidepressants) are of no value in characterological depressions as those I described, these antidepressants are not addictive. The danger of addiction is when drugs such as the benzodiazepines (for example, Xanax, Tranxene, Ativan, and Valium) are used for depression. The tranquilizing drugs that are often prescribed may indeed temporarily relieve an addict's symptoms of depression just as the alcohol or other chemicals did, but they carry a very high risk of addiction in themselves. Unwittingly, the doctor may have substituted one addiction for another.

An addictive thinker may suffer chronic dissatisfaction. This could be due to unrealistic expectations rather than actual deprivation. This person may need the help of a therapist in clarifying reality. A most effective therapy can be a group experience, where, under the guidance of a skilled therapist, an addict can begin identifying with others in the group and observing their distortions. The addict may become aware that he or she, too, has been distorting reality. Seeing other people who also had unrealistic expectations can help the addict become aware of his or her own equally unrealistic expectations. Perhaps the real world isn't all dazzling colors, but it isn't all drab and gray either.

The addicted person has often shut off an entire feeling system to avoid certain unpleasant feelings. As the addict is helped to realize this, he or she begins to understand that much of the darkness and gray was due to a sensory blockage. As the person becomes more comfortable with feelings and dismantles this massive defense system, he or she begins to appreciate some of the color and excitement that does exist in the world.

Nothing prevents an addict from having a clinical depression. However, diagnosing a clinical depression in a person who is in early recovery may be extremely difficult because the symptoms of depression may be due to an underlying depressive attitude that emerges after cessation of chemical use.

At the present time, we do not have a laboratory test that can diagnose a biochemical disorder, and the diagnosis must be made on the basis of the doctor's evaluation. It is therefore important that the doctor be familiar with addictive diseases as well as clinical depression, in order to make a proper evaluation and judgment.

When Both Are Present

People who have only a clinical depression and are not addicts can be treated effectively with antidepressants and psychotherapy. People who are addicts and do not have a clinical depression will be helped by a recovery program and counseling. If a person has both addiction and clinical depression, both treatments are necessary. Antidepressants are not a substitute for a recovery program, nor is the recovery program a substitute for antidepressant medication. Appropriate use of both can result in an all-around recovery.

If an addict is diagnosed with a clinical depression and the doctor prescribes an antidepressant, there should be no hesitancy in taking this medication. Some people in recovery may say that taking any mind-altering drug is a violation of sobriety. While this may be true for addictive kinds of tranquilizers (with rare exception), it is not true of antidepressants or of mood stabilizers such as lithium. These can be used safely by a recovering addict.

Some people may have tried antidepressant medication during active addiction and found that it was not helpful. This may have been due to the interference by alcohol or other drugs. Once abstinence has been achieved, the antidepressant may be effective.

18

Must One Reach Bottom?

True recovery from addiction means more than simple abstinence. It means relinquishing the pathological thought system and adopting a healthy one. Since addiction involves a distortion of perception, only some major event or series of events can make the addict question the validity of his or her perception. The event or events that bring about this breakthrough are sometimes referred to as a rock-bottom experience.

The Meaning of Rock Bottom

The term *rock bottom* has been traditionally used and is still widely used in the addiction field, so it is just as well to preserve it. However, it should be clarified. "Rock bottom" does not necessarily mean total desocialization, loss of family, or loss of employment; it does not mean utter disaster. All it means is that something has occurred in the life of the addict that has sufficient impact to make the addict wish to change at least part of his or her lifestyle.

In recent years, many businesses have implemented an employee assistance program (EAP). When an employee seems to have a problem that is affecting work performance, he or she is asked to see a counselor. If the problem is chemical dependency, the employee is then referred for further evaluation and treatment. It may be implicit or explicit that an employee who refuses to seek help and continues to perform poorly will be dismissed. For many men and women, this referral has constituted a rock bottom, and they have entered a treatment program ten or twenty years earlier than they would have otherwise. Without the rock bottom of feeling their job in jeopardy, they might have progressed further to more dire consequences.

Because of the increased awareness of chemical dependency in adolescents, most young people entering treatment have suffered few of the consequences of advanced addiction. For them, rock bottom is the desire to remain in the home and maintain a relationship with their parents.

As you will see, the variability in what constitutes a rock-bottom experience may be explained by the law of human gravity.

The Law of Human Gravity

A law of human behavior that appears as inviolable as the law of gravity might well be called the "law of human gravity": A person will gravitate from a condition that *appears* to be one of greater distress to a condition that *appears* to be one of lesser distress, and never in the reverse direction. According to this law, it is impossible for a person to choose greater distress. Any attempt to reverse the direction of the choice will be as futile as trying to make water flow uphill.

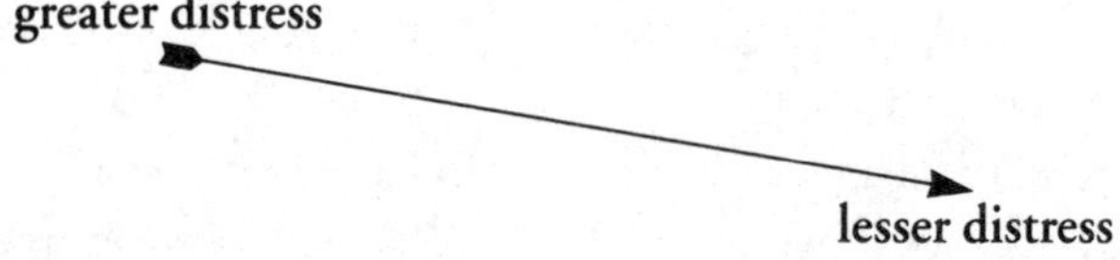

Alcohol and other mind-altering chemicals provide some measure of relief from discomfort, whether this is relief from anxiety, depression, loneliness, self-consciousness, or just the compulsive urge. Abstinence, at least initially, causes distress, sometimes psychological discomfort, and often severe physical discomfort.

If we try to get addicted people to stop alcohol or other chemical use, we are essentially asking them to choose a greater distress. But it is beyond human capacity to choose a greater distress. From this analysis it might appear that we should stop all efforts at treatment! Treatment can't work! But we know for a fact that treatment does work and that people do achieve sobriety. How does this happen?

Achieving Sobriety through Changes in Perception

While the law of human gravity is inviolable, and the direction can never change, it is possible for people to change their *perceptions.* People can learn to see chemical use as the greater distress and abstinence as the lesser distress.

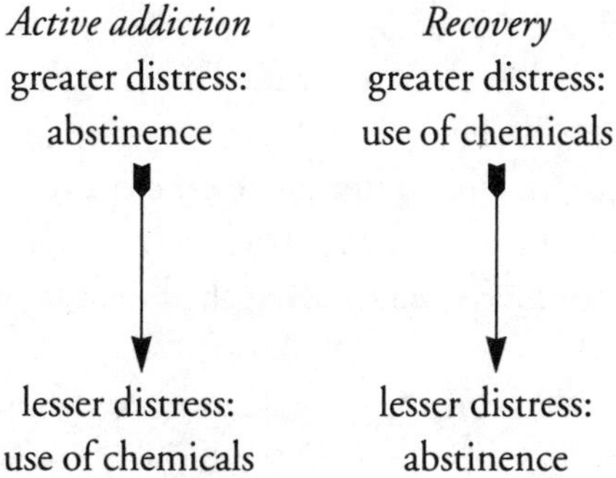

How does this change of perception come about? All mind-altering chemicals sooner or later cause some kind of discomfort:

- the loss of respect from family and friends
- the threat of losing a job
- poor school performance
- severe gastrointestinal symptoms
- hangovers
- hallucinations
- falls and bruises

- convulsive seizures
- the distress of poor memory
- the threat of imprisonment
- the terror of delusions

When any of these, alone or in combination, reach the critical point—where the misery equals or exceeds whatever relief the chemical provides—then the person's perception of what is a greater or lesser distress changes.

This, then, is what happens when rock bottom occurs. *Rock bottom is nothing more than a change of perception, where abstinence is seen as a lesser distress than use of chemicals.* If at any time after abstinence is achieved, even many years later, abstinence becomes the greater distress, relapse will occur.

The natural course of addiction is such that rock bottom will come if no one interferes. But people in the addict's environment, with every good intention, may remove some of the distresses that the chemical produces. For example, a co-worker may cover for a colleague who is hung over. This prevents a change in perception of greater and lesser distress and permits the active addiction to continue. This is why people who remove the distressful consequences of chemical use are referred to as *enablers.*

Remember, allowing the natural unpleasant consequences to occur is not the same as punishing the user. *Punishing* is inflicting pain from the outside. If, for example, a drinker sees marriage as the source of distress, he or she will separate rather than quit drinking. Only when the alcoholic discovers that the drinking is causing the misery will sobriety become a solution.

Addicts' perceptions also change when they see the rewards of abstinence. When the rewards of abstinence begin to exceed the rewards of mind-altering chemicals, addicts can change their perceptions of which is the greater or lesser distress.

Meeting people who have sobriety and seeing that they are happy and productive demonstrates the rewards of abstinence.

Getting a positive response to sobriety from family, friends, and colleagues is a reward. Regaining self-esteem is a reward. Retaining one's job is a reward.

The active addict may recognize all these as rewards yet feel they are beyond reach. This is where competent therapy, with realistic and appropriate self-esteem building, can make a difference. With proper help, the addict may begin to believe that these rewards are achievable and perceive abstinence as the lesser distress.

People vary greatly in their perceptions of rewards of misery. A therapist can learn what each person defines as *rewards* and *distress* in order to help the person put addiction and abstinence in proper perspective. The combination of rock-bottom experiences plus realistic anticipation of the benefits of abstinence can make sobriety possible.

19

Addictive Thinkers and Trust

Treatment professionals and others can use many techniques to gain the trust of an addict, but, whatever the method, successful treatment depends on the addict's trust.

Let's realize what we are asking of the addicted person. First, we are asking this person to completely and permanently abstain from use of the chemical that has made life livable, maybe the *only* thing that has made it tolerable. This is a very big thing to ask of someone.

A bright, recovering sales rep said to me on the tenth anniversary of his sobriety, "Doctor, when I was in detox and you showed me my physical exam and the lab tests, and you explained that if I didn't stop drinking I would soon die, that didn't faze me. I would have chosen to drink and to die. I could not conceive of living without alcohol when I needed it."

Abstinence is often a formidable challenge. But even abstinence is not recovery, only a *prerequisite* to recovery. Recovery requires a change in attitude and behavior, which means a change in the way the addicted person thinks and has thought for most of his or her life. It means overcoming addictive thinking. The formula can be shown as follows:

Recovery = Abstinence + Change

The Difficulty of Reasoning with Addicts

Think, for a moment, what would happen if someone you trusted told you to take something precious, such as a fine crystal vase or a valuable porcelain sculpture, and drop it from a fourth-floor window onto a sidewalk below. You might say, "Are you crazy? That's a family heirloom. It's priceless to me. Why should I do such a foolish thing and break it?"

Imagine your friend replying, "Aha! That's where you're wrong. You see, you've been operating under this delusion that there is a law of gravity and that when you let go of things they fall downward. But you've been the victim of deception. There is no such thing as a law of gravity. Trust me, my friend. You'll see that if you extend that vase or sculpture out the window and let go of it, it will not drop to the ground. It will remain suspended in the air, and you can retrieve it anytime you wish."

No doubt you will conclude that your trusted friend has flipped. *The poor person is insane!* you tell yourself. *I have always known that when I let go of things they do fall, and there is a law of gravity. This poor lunatic friend of mine is trying to convince me of the greatest absurdity. How crazy can a person get?*

When we try to convince addicts of the fallacy of their thinking, it is like telling someone that his or her belief in the law of gravity is a delusion. It is the height of futility to expect an addictive thinker to abandon that concept of reality and accept ours instead.

Two Essential Factors in Recovery

How, then, can recovery ever occur? There are two essential factors.

1. *Addicts Must Lose Faith in Their Current Reasoning Power.* Addicts must learn that their concept of reality and thought processes are distorted. Unfortunately, others can do little to cause the addicted person to doubt a lifelong thinking pattern. The only thing that will cause the addict to doubt is a rock-bottom experience—any event that can make the addict reconsider his or her behavior

and attitude. At such time, a therapist or professional can move in and say, "Look, you are becoming aware that your perception of reality is incorrect and that your ways of thinking have been distorted. I will help you discover a valid system of thinking."

2. *Addicts Must Accept the Possibility of Another Version of Reality from Someone They Trust.* I try to help patients in treatment understand this "reality check" by giving them the example of an excellent cook who has always cooked by tasting, never by following the recipe. The person doesn't pay attention to measuring ingredients. After putting in the ingredients, the cook tastes the concoction and adds salt, sugar, lemon, and spices, tasting the mixture periodically, always adding what is missing until it tastes right.

But what happens if this person develops a severe head cold with clogged sinuses and is unable to taste anything? Since the cook doesn't rely on measurements, the next best thing is to call someone and ask, "Could you please taste this for me and tell me what you think it needs? I have a bad cold and my taste is off."

For addicts, a treatment staff can provide this function. The addict's "taste buds" for assessing reality are not functioning properly. A treatment professional can help the addict to assess reality and develop a correct system of thinking.

Developing Trust in Treatment

Isn't it a bit much to expect the addict to trust a person he or she has never seen before?

Most addicts lack an ability to trust. If they grew up in the home of an alcoholic parent, they had little opportunity to learn trust. Home may have been filled with lies and deception.

The drinking parent lied to the sober parent; the sober parent deceived the drinking parent. Most children of alcoholics have learned that no one can be trusted.

Even children who grew up in healthy, functioning homes may have problems trusting others. Parents are not always forthright with their children for many reasons. Parents often think a child can't understand some things. So, instead of telling the truth, they concoct something they think the child can grasp.

An addict who encounters a treatment professional may have little reason to trust. The rock-bottom experience may have pulled the foundation from beneath the addict, who feels suspended as if in midair. A treatment staff person shakes hands with the addict and says, "We will try to help you." *Big deal!*

If addicts have so little trust, how do they accept treatment from doctors or dentists? Or submit themselves to surgery? The answer is that these professional helpers are not saying things that contradict what the addict already believes. The dentist says the addict's wisdom tooth is impacted and must be removed; the addict never believed that an impacted wisdom tooth should *not* be removed.

Treatment for chemical addiction is different. The addict will have to begin thinking in new ways in recovery, and that calls for profound trust.

Addicts in treatment must have reason to believe they won't be misled, that their welfare is the prime goal of treatment, and that nothing can deter the staff from that goal. Treatment staff may seek alliances with the addict's family, employer, or the court system, but only with the client's knowledge.

People in treatment for chemical dependency test those treating them, as well they should. Treatment staff tell them that much, if not everything, they believed until now is wrong, that their thinking has been distorted and is incorrect, and that they should rely on someone else's thinking.

In the past, residential treatment programs typically lasted four weeks. Many years of addictive thinking can't be reversed in twenty-eight days, but at least the addict had a head start while in a chemical-free environment. Today, with outpatient treatment essentially replacing residential treatment, most addicts do not have the benefit of this protected period.

The restriction of residential treatment has presented a challenge to therapists, who, like their clients, are compelled to deal with a new reality. Outpatient programs have risen to the challenge. With alcohol and opiate addiction, enforcement of abstinence has been enhanced by wider use of Disulfiram and naltrexone. Contracts have been written with clients, and therapists have developed additional skills to help addicts survive the post-acute withdrawal phase.

Although the traditional twenty-eight-day residential treatment program has been replaced, intensive outpatient treatment is usually of a longer duration. This allows the therapist a bit longer time to help the addict make the transition from addictive thinking to normal thinking.

Failure to Address Addictive Thinking

Let's say a newly sober addict leaves a treatment program after a period of enforced abstinence in which he or she has overcome physical withdrawal. Immediately resuming use of alcohol or other drugs indicates that the person did not begin to change his or her addictive thinking. No person thinking clearly would want to promptly return to active addiction. The only possible conclusion is that the person *remained in addictive thinking.*

This, in turn, almost always means that the therapist was unable to gain the trust of the client. This is not necessarily a reflection on the therapist's skills and dedication; the person may have entered treatment with a deep sense of distrust and is unable to trust anyone—yet. Or, in spite of all that has happened, the person may not yet have reached the particular rock-bottom experience that could begin to break down addictive thinking. It is generally a matter of time before the addict realizes that the therapist was right and that his or her own thinking has been faulty. The addict then usually returns to treatment, this time with a greater trust in the therapist.

What has been said about trust applies to everyone who wishes to relate to the addict constructively. This includes not only the therapist but also family members, employer, pastor, sponsor, and friends in the recovery program. Each can earn trust, respect it, and guard it carefully.

20

Spirituality and Spiritual Emptiness

Although almost every human disease can be found among animals, there is little evidence that animals in their normal habitat develop addictive diseases. Some animals whose brains have been treated with certain chemicals may eat or drink excessively, but this does not occur in animals in their normal environments. Indulgence in excesses appears to be a uniquely human phenomenon. Why?

In contrast to animals, which have only physical urges and desire, human beings crave spiritual fulfillment as well. When this spiritual need goes unmet, humans feel vague unrest. While hunger, thirst, or the sex drive are easily identified, spiritual craving is harder to recognize and fulfill. People may feel that something is missing, but not know what that something is.

It should not come as a surprise that spirituality, too, is subject to addictive distortion.*

Filling the Spiritual Emptiness

Most people learn through experience that certain substances produce a sense of gratification. Consequently, addictive thinking can lead people to try to quench this vague spiritual craving through food or drugs or sex or money. These objects may give some gratification, but they do nothing to solve the basic prob-

* The ideas discussed in this chapter are from *Animals and Angels: Spirituality and Recovery* by Abraham J. Twerski (Center City, Minn.: Hazelden Educational Materials, 1990).

lem: the unmet spiritual needs. The feeling of satisfaction disappears soon, replaced by longing.

Think of it this way. Humans require certain amounts of vitamins A, B complex, C, D, E, and K to function normally. A lack of any of these vitamins will result in specific deficiency syndromes, such as scurvy with vitamin C deficiency or beriberi with vitamin B-1 deficiency. If a person lacks vitamin B-1 and is given massive doses of vitamin C, the deficiency disease will remain unchanged. Nothing can change until the specific vitamin needed is supplied. You cannot compensate for a deficiency of one vitamin with excess of another.

This is similar to the mistake addicts make. The addictive thinker reasons that since food or sex or money or alcohol or other drugs have satisfied *some* cravings, they will satisfy other needs.

This also helps us understand the phenomenon of switching *addictions;* for instance, switching an eating disorder for compulsive gambling, or switching sexual addiction for workaholism.

Many recovering people have said, "During periods of abstinence, I felt some kind of void inside of me. I had no idea what that was all about. Now I know that that was an empty space where God belonged."

The Meaning of Spirituality

Why is it that we can easily identify that food satisfies hunger and that water satisfies thirst, but we can't readily identify what satisfies spiritual cravings?

There is an answer, which theologians consider to be the core of what humankind is all about: A human being is not just another animal, differing only in degree of intelligence. Humans, as morally free beings, can choose whether to recognize their spirituality and their unique relationship with God.

But what if a person does not have a religious orientation,

and "God as we understand Him" is the support group? Does the lack of formal religious belief preclude spirituality?

Not at all. Humans are different than other animals. In addition to greater intelligence, humans also possess a number of characteristics that animals do not have. For example, we have the capacity to learn from history, and animals obviously do not. We can contemplate the purpose of existence. We can think of ways to better ourselves and can implement them. We can delay gratification and think about the long-term consequences of our actions. Finally, we have the capacity to make moral decisions, which may result in denying ourselves behaviors that our bodies lust for.

All these capacities that are unique to humans may be said to constitute the *spirit.* The spirit, then, is that part of the human being that distinguishes us from other forms of life. A religionist will say that the spirit was instilled in humanity at the time of creation. An atheist might say that it developed over the millions of years of evolution. But few deny that humans have these capacities, hence that humans have a spirit.

When we exercise these unique human capacities, we are being *spiritual.* It is possible, therefore, to be spiritual without being religious, because nowhere among these unique human capacities is it a requisite to be religious.

We can also understand the importance of spirituality in recovery from addiction. Active addicts obviously have not learned from the history of their past behavior, because they repeat actions that have been proven to be destructive. Their purpose in life is to get high, so addicts seek no other purpose. They can hardly consider self-improvement when their behavior is frankly self-destructive. Active addicts cannot delay gratification and do not consider the consequences of their actions. Finally, addicts lack freedom, being ruthlessly dominated by the compulsion of the addiction. Addiction is thus the antithesis of spirituality.

Addictive thinking is nonspiritual, since its goal is the polar opposite of spirituality. This is why recovery from addiction requires a shift from addictive thinking to spirituality, although not necessarily to religion. Certainly religion embraces spirituality, and may be an additional source of strength in recovery, but it is not absolutely essential for recovery.

21

Addictive Thinking and Relapse

A recurrence of addictive thinking often *precedes* relapse into drinking or use of other chemicals. Distorted thinking can also *follow* relapse as a person attempts to return to a Twelve Step program.

Growth in Recovery

Because recovery is a growth process, relapse is an interruption of that growth. But relapse does *not* mean going back to square one. Yet almost without exception, that is what the relapser is likely to think. After two years or twelve years of recovery, a person who relapses may feel back at rock bottom. This conclusion is mistaken, however, and can negatively affect recovery from a relapse. Many people who relapse think, *What's the use? I've tried and it doesn't work. I might as well give up the fight.*

The problem is, they are beginning with a conclusion rather than looking at the facts of their situation: the progress they've made, the skills they've learned, the rewards of recovery. Instead, the person who has relapsed wishes to continue the use of chemicals. The ideas of futility and despair are nothing but typical addictive thinking, the purpose of which is to promote continued use of chemicals. The correct conclusion, as the following story illustrates, is that relapse doesn't wipe out the gains recovering addicts have made to that point.

Slippery Spots

One winter day I had a package to mail at the post office. My car battery was dead, and I had to walk eight blocks to the post office. I tried to watch for slippery spots on the sidewalk, but, in spite of my caution, I slipped and fell hard. While I fortunately did not break any bones, I did feel a jolting pain.

I may or may not have uttered a few expletives at the person who should have shoveled the sidewalk more thoroughly. But I knew that whether I fell because of the deceptive appearance of the sidewalk or my negligence, I was not going to get to the post office unless I got up and walked, pain and all. As I limped on, I was even more alert for possible slippery spots that might bring about another fall.

In spite of my painful fall, I was two blocks closer to my destination than when I had started. The fall did not erase the progress I had made.

This is how we can view relapse. Regardless of its pain, relapse is *not* a regression back to square one. The progress made up to the point of the relapse can't be denied. An addict who relapses must start from that point and, as with the icy slip, be even more alert to those things that can cause relapse.

Relapse of Thinking

A shrewd observer, whether therapist or sponsor, may detect a recurrence of addictive thinking that is likely to result in relapse. If this is corrected, relapse may be forestalled. For example, a recovering person who begins exhibiting signs of impatience has likely slipped back into the addict's concept of time. Someone who claims not to need as many meetings because she is now in control is probably back into omnipotence. Someone wallowing in remorse may be regressing into shame. Someone who reverts to rationalizing or projecting blame, or who becomes unusually sensitive to other people's behavior, may be experiencing the hypersensitivity or self-righteousness of the addict. Becoming morose or pessimistic can signal the depression or the morbid expectations characteristic of addictive thinking. Any recurrence of what we have come to recognize as addictive thinking may be a prelude to relapse. Prompt detection of the relapse into addictive thinking and reinstitution of healthy thinking may help the addict avoid the chemical relapse.

Reentering a Twelve Step Program

Many people become frustrated on returning to AA, NA, or another Twelve Step program after a relapse. They remember the wonderful feeling, the glow, and the warmth they experienced on entering the program the first time and are disappointed when they don't get this feeling on reentry.

But there is only one first kiss. The experience can never be duplicated. On first entering the Twelve Step program, addicts find others like themselves. They are made to feel welcome and comfortable as they become part of the recovery population. The person returning to the program looking for this feeling will likely be frustrated and disappointed. It won't feel so fresh and new.

Cocaine addicts say that throughout their addiction they tried in vain to recapture the high of their first use, but they could never do it. Attempting to reexperience the first high of recovery is quite similar.

Remember this, for it is important: *Be realistic about relapse.* The growth in sobriety that preceded relapse is not lost, and a person can't expect the original experience in recovery the second time around. These are two facts that addictive thinking often distorts.

22

The Frustrations of Growth

Frustration is not the cause of alcoholism or other drug addiction. Many people have learned to tolerate frustration and somehow manage without escaping into the anesthesia of chemicals. People who do use chemicals to manage may have not learned how to tolerate frustration well. Perhaps they can manage some frustrations, but in their addictive thinking have great difficulty with others.

We become frustrated when we feel that things could and should be different than they are. When we know things are happening as could be expected, we do not become frustrated, even if we do not particularly like what is happening.

A Series of Challenges

What addictive thinkers often don't realize is that life is a series of ongoing challenges. We may put forth a great deal of effort to overcome one hurdle. No sooner do we begin to relax than we find ourselves confronting another hurdle, and this goes on ad infinitum.

Addictive thinkers may believe that there is something unusual about this. If they find themselves unable to go an extended period without some disturbance of their peace, they feel singled out and unjustly harassed. If they drink or use other chemicals, they will point to an intolerable series of problems with which they must try to cope. *It's just one thing after another,* they tell themselves. *Never a moment of peace.*

Although a legitimate complaint, this happens to be reality

for most people. The addict is not apt to be aware of this, however. The way the addict sees it, no one else could possibly be subject to such terrible stresses and problems.

People close to the addict might know enough not to believe that the person has a legitimate excuse to use alcohol or other drugs. But they could be inadvertently lured into unhealthy empathy. The various problems the addict describes may sound like too much for anyone to bear. On closer analysis, though, an addict's problems are not that different from the nonaddict's problems. But the addictive thinker's perception is that they are radically different: *Other people get a break once in a while, but not me. Never.*

Recovering addicts may bring their unrealistic expectations into sobriety. They may believe that other people in recovery have had an easier time. *My problems are the worst,* they think. *My spouse used to complain when I drank, and now I hear about my going to meetings every night. The supervisor watches me like a hawk. My old friends don't call anymore. . . .* As recovering addicts come into regular contact with others in recovery, however, they begin to see that everyone else doesn't have it better and, in fact, other people are a lot like they are.

Every aspect of recovery is subject to growth. Accepting life on its own terms, accepting powerlessness, surrendering to a Higher Power, taking and sharing a moral inventory, making amends—all these take place gradually. A person who has been recovering for several years may look back on early recovery and see how much there was to learn, how far he or she has come.

Growing Pains

A recovering alcoholic complained to me about the constant frustrations and crises she faced. As we examined them, it turned out that each crisis consisted of new demands being made on her. These additional demands were being made because she was doing well at her current level—each crisis was a take-off point for further growth.

"But this is so painful," she complained.

"Of course," I responded. "Haven't you ever heard of growing pains?"

"Well, how long do I have to keep growing?"

"We should all keep growing until we die," I said.

Another woman in recovery put it so succinctly. "They told me that if I stopped drinking, things would get better. Well, they were wrong. *Things* did not get better. *I* got better."

Some of the problems that go along with chemical use may indeed disappear with sobriety, but many problems of reality persist. For most people, economic survival is a struggle. Things may happen in the economy which are beyond our control, which may threaten our livelihood. Also, we are all subject to illness and disease. Our children are apt to have problems with school, friends, and, yes, even drugs. There is no dearth of problems in the reality that everyone confronts, and there is no reason for addicts to expect problems to disappear just because they became sober. What happens, however, is that recovering addicts begin to recognize their strengths at coping with these various challenges. Furthermore, if they need some help to deal with them, they have learned where to find help and how to accept it.

Only the Beginning

Many people naively believe that they have completed their course in recovery when they "graduate" from a treatment program. At that point, it is difficult for them to understand that they have not yet even *begun* recovery. The treatment program is only an introduction; recovery is yet to come.

One of the worst things that can happen to a person who emerges from a treatment program is for everything to run smoothly for several weeks. This reinforces the fantasy that life can be devoid of challenges. The person begins to think how easy recovery is because those vexing problems are no longer occurring. When the inevitable problems do occur, the person is caught off guard.

I tell the residents at our rehabilitation center that if they encounter difficulties in the first few weeks after discharge, they can blame me. I pray that they should *not* have things go too smoothly for the first few weeks because I want recovering addicts to encounter real life and experience the pressures of reality immediately. I want them to promptly use the tools they have been given during treatment:

- to call their sponsor
- to attend meetings
- to share with others, and
- to follow other recommendations

Addictive thinkers may think they deserve to rest after their strenuous effort in treatment, but this kind of thinking can lead to relapse. Hurdles in the path are inevitable, and it is realistic to expect them in recovery.

23

Ridiculous Explanations, Sensible Solutions

When we see addictive people behave irrationally, we are often so stunned that we don't know how to react. We are much like the farmer who for the first time in his life sees a giraffe in the zoo and says, "I see it, but I don't believe it." *It is obvious that what addicts are doing is destructive to themselves and others,* we think, *so why aren't addicts able to relate their behavior to alcohol and other chemicals?*

When a psychotic person behaves insanely, it does not cause us to lose our bearings. But when a person who is otherwise perfectly sane and rational does crazy things, we are often taken aback. We may begin to doubt our senses, asking ourselves, *Could it be that what I see is really happening?* This self-doubt may be so intense that we are vulnerable to accepting the most ridiculous explanations as being sensible!

The addictive person's thinking processes may be so affected by the action of chemicals on the brain that the wildest self-contradictions and inconsistencies in behavior are understandable. Indeed, when addicted people recover and look back at the irrational behavior, they are frequently amazed at how they thought and acted. What is less understandable is how and why the significant others in the addict's environment, whose minds are unaltered by chemicals, fall prey to so much distorted thought and behavior.

The answer is that all of us have unique needs, some healthy, some not so healthy, and the emotional pressure to gratify these needs can greatly affect the way we think and feel. Sometimes these emotional pressures can distort our thinking almost or just as much as the chemical used by the addict.

This is why the concept of addictive thinking is so important to understand. Addictive thinking exists and operates in every addicted person and, to a greater or lesser degree, in the significant others.

Testing Reality

In ordinary life, no one stops to ask, *Is it possible that I am hallucinating?* We cannot function well in reality if we doubt everything. When the bus arrives at the bus stop, we get on the bus and do not think, *Maybe this bus does not really exist. Maybe I'm just hallucinating a bus.* Such thinking would paralyze us.

When things occur that are totally beyond our expectations, we may pinch ourselves to be sure that we are not dreaming. This can occur when anything out of the ordinary happens, whether it is something good or terrible. We pinch ourselves to test reality.

It may be asking too much of active addicts to try to discover whether their perceptions are real or distorted. But people whose brains are unaffected by chemicals and who relate to a chemical user would be wise to check out their own thinking, as well as put the addict's behavior in proper perspective. This holds true whether we are a husband, wife, parent, child, therapist, supervisor, friend, pastor, or anyone else relating to an active addict. The more we understand how addicts think and function, the less likely we are to be paralyzed by the shock of their behavior, and the less likely we are to be taken in by their ingenious cunning and manipulation. Furthermore, if we can grasp that there are powerful forces within ourselves that are capable of producing many of the same distortions that result from chemicals, we may be less resistant when our role as codependents is pointed out to us.

Two Plus Two Equals Five

The mother of a young man who was destroying himself with alcohol and other drugs could not understand how he could be oblivious to the disastrous effects that chemicals were having on his life. She asked for help in dealing with him. "But don't tell me I have to put him out of the house or that I should not bail him out of jail," she said. "I don't want to hear that."

I responded, "Please tell me how much is two plus two, but don't say four."

She had been unable to see that her own thinking was no less distorted than her son's. Why was her thinking distorted? Because when she bailed him out of jail or didn't put him out of the house, she enabled him to go on using chemicals without seeing the magnitude of the problem. She kept him from his rock-bottom experience from which recovery would be possible.

Not a New Concept

If you read the literature on addiction, addictive thinking will jump out at you from every page.

Is severe pain normal? No. Is it normal for a person with a fractured leg to be in severe pain? Yes.

Is fever normal? No. Is it normal for a person with an infection to have a high fever? Yes.

Is addictive thinking normal? No. Is it normal for chemically dependent people and codependents to have addictive thinking? Yes.

Since you are reading this book, you are, in one way or another, concerned about addiction. As such, you can be vulnerable to addictive thinking. Check this out with someone who can take a more objective look at your life. With the help of another, you will be better able to clarify your own reality.

Select Bibliography

Beattie, Melody. *Codependent No More.* Center City, Minn.: Hazelden, 1987, 1992.

Branden, Nathaniel. *The Power of Self-Esteem.* Deerfield Beach, Fla.: Health Communications, 1992.

Gorski, Terence, and Merlene Miller. *Staying Sober.* Independence, Mo.: Herald House/Independence Press, 1986.

Lindquist, Marie. *Holding Back: Why We Hide the Truth about Ourselves.* Center City, Minn.: Hazelden, 1987.

Nakken, Craig. *The Addictive Personality.* Center City, Minn.: Hazelden, 1988, 1996.

One Day at a Time in Al-Anon. New York: Al-Anon Family Group Headquarters, 1986.

Rosellini, Gayle, and Mark Worden. *Of Course You're Angry.* Center City, Minn.: Hazelden, 1987, 1997.

Sedlak, David. "Childhood: Setting the Stage for Addiction in Childhood and Adolescence." In *Adolescent Substance Abuse: A Guide to Prevention and Treatment,* edited by Richard Isralowitz and Mark Singer. New York: Haworth Press, 1983.

Twelve Steps and Twelve Traditions. 38th ed. New York: Alcoholics Anonymous World Services, Inc., 1988.

Twenty-Four Hours a Day. Rev. ed. Center City, Minn.: Hazelden, 1975.

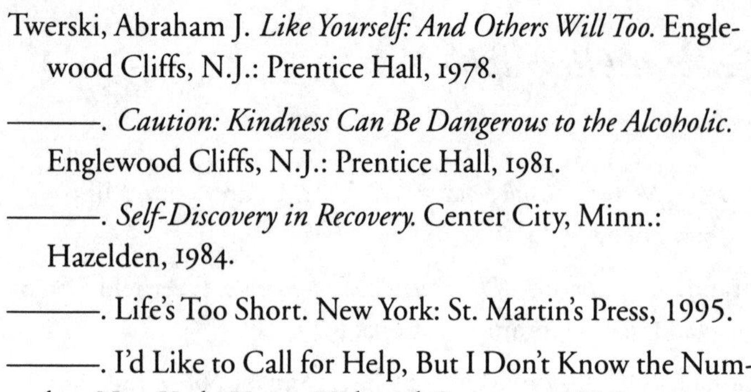

Twerski, Abraham J. *Like Yourself: And Others Will Too.* Englewood Cliffs, N.J.: Prentice Hall, 1978.

———. *Caution: Kindness Can Be Dangerous to the Alcoholic.* Englewood Cliffs, N.J.: Prentice Hall, 1981.

———. *Self-Discovery in Recovery.* Center City, Minn.: Hazelden, 1984.

———. Life's Too Short. New York: St. Martin's Press, 1995.

———. I'd Like to Call for Help, But I Don't Know the Number. New York: Henry Holt and Company, 1996.

Index